Making Connections with Writing

AN EXPRESSIVE WRITING MODEL IN JAPANESE SCHOOLS

Mary M. Kitagawa

Tucson Unified School District

Chisato Kitagawa

University of Arizona

With a Foreword by Ken Goodman

HEINEMANN / PORTSMOUTH, NEW HAMPSHIRE

HEINEMANN EDUCATIONAL BOOKS, INC.
70 Court Street   Portsmouth, NH 03801

LONDON EDINBURGH MELBOURNE AUCKLAND
SINGAPORE NEW DELHI IBADAN NAIROBI
JOHANNESBURG KINGSTON PORT OF SPAIN

10 9 8 7 6 5 4 3 2 1

Library of Congress Cataloging-in-Publication Data

Kitagawa, Mary M.
  Making connections with writing.

  Bibliography: p.
  Includes index.
  1. Japanese language—Composition and exercises.
2. Japanese language—Study and teaching (Elementary)—
Japan. 3. Language arts (Elementary)—Japan.
I. Kitagawa, Chisato. II. Title.
LB1577.J3K527   1987   372.6′5′956   86-29406
ISBN 0-435-08437-2

Photos by Kristen S. Kitagawa.
Designed by Wladislaw Finne.
Printed in the United States of America.

Dedicated to our parents:
William, Vera, Chiaki, and Sumi

CONTENTS

FOREWORD *by Kenneth S. Goodman*

When Mary Kitagawa first shared with me her discovery of a movement among Japanese teachers to encourage children to write from
their own experience, I was intrigued but must admit that, drawing on
my own schema, I equated it with elements of language-experience
approaches to teaching reading in the United States. From her subsequent articles I learned that it was much more than that. So I was
very pleased when she told me of the plans she and her husband,
Chisato Kitagawa, had made to spend an extended time in Japan
studying *seikatsu tsuzurikata.*

This book, which reports the findings of their study, would be valuable
to teachers in the English-speaking world even if it only showed what
it is possible for a grass-roots movement of dedicated teachers to
accomplish. Sometimes under very adverse circumstances, these teachers
committed themselves to helping their pupils cope with life and the
world around them through writing. In the dark hours of World War
II the militarists in Japan saw this commitment as a threat, and the
movement was crushed through the persecution and arrest of 135
teachers, some of whom died as a result of their experiences. Still, the
movement survived and spread. A network of small circles of teachers
thrives in Japan today. Through it, teachers use their shared interest
in seikatsu to improve themselves and their effectiveness with their
pupils. They learn from their pupils as they support their pupils as
learners.

But seikatsu tsuzurikata has important lessons for teachers everywhere.
In this view, "It is the writer, not the product, that the writing process
nurtures. The philosophy focuses on an outcome defined in terms of
beneficial effects upon the writer-self more than the text-producing
capabilities of a potential author" (p. 12). John Dewey talked about
learning from experience. Seikatsu teachers believe they can help
learners examine and come to grips with their experience through writing.
So this is not simply a method for developing writing. It becomes the
essence of the curriculum. Reading grows from writing, and through
writing children come to understand themselves and their world.

As the Kitagawas point out, there is much in this Japanese philosophy
that teachers participating in the whole-language movement in the

English-speaking countries will find immediately useful. It is process rather than product oriented; it accepts the egocentrism of young learners as a place to begin; it sees language development as an intrinsic part of using language to cope with experience; it sees teachers as supporting self-initiated learning. All teachers will find the Kitagawas' documentation of how teachers respond to pupils' writing most informative. Nothing is more important to the seikatsu teachers than the comments they make on their pupils' papers, and their circle meetings focus on criticism of each other's efforts.

Making Connections with Writing will also be useful to those interested in teacher effectiveness. The movement illustrates the importance of teachers developing a belief system based on examination of their responsibility to learners and knowledge of content and pedagogy. It demonstrates the importance of personal commitment and peer interaction in professional development.

Researchers, particularly those who do ethnographic research in classrooms and those who engage in text analysis, will find new concepts in seikatsu to consider in their analyses. Evaluators of writing may learn from seikatsu to build more respect for process and development into their efforts.

Perhaps more than anything, teachers who read this book will feel a little more pride in being part of a profession of universal importance.

PREFACE

Seikatsu tsuzurikata (pronounced SAY-KAH-TSOO TSOO-ZOO-REE-KAH-TAH) 'life experience composition'—or, for ease of reference, *seikatsu* (SAY-KAH-TSOO)—is a philosophically oriented writing education movement that has been practiced in various parts of Japan by zealous schoolteachers for some sixty years. As a topic for research, it can be many things to many people. In Japan it has been characterized variously as, for example, a remarkably successful case of Japanese pragmatism, a manifestation of a uniquely Japanese approach to community building in school, or a curriculum given to whole person education. And, while the name *seikatsu tsuzurikata* is not a household word in Japan today, books and articles on seikatsu abound, both by proponents of the movement and by nonparticipant researchers in various disciplinary fields. Interestingly, the movement is hardly known outside of Japan, despite its considerable importance in the history of modern Japan and its potential contribution to the theory of writing education in the world. A plausible explanation for this is that seikatsu belongs essentially to the classroom teachers in Japan who have adopted it out of devotion to their students. They have neither time nor use for purely abstract academic discourse. It is a grass-roots movement, propagated by those who choose to dedicate themselves to a grass-roots cause. In this sense, the universal appeal of seikatsu may best be appreciated by fellow classroom teachers, even from different cultural contexts.

This classroom perspective is the one we, a husband and wife team, a native-speaking Japanese linguist at an American university and an American elementary-school teacher, have adopted throughout our study of seikatsu philosophy, methodology, and international significance. We spent an intensive seven months doing research on the seikatsu curriculum in action in Japan and engaged in a fair amount of reading on the subject before and after. Although the two of us have worked together on the project with equal enthusiasm, the "camera angle" adopted for reporting this research is that of an elementary-school teacher in America who is especially interested in writing education. Accordingly, chapter 17 uses the pronoun "I" to highlight Mary's perspective and experience as an elementary-school teacher. Other chapters refer to us individually in the third person, "Mary" or "Chisato," where necessary. Otherwise, the pronoun "we" is used to refer to our shared perception as joint authors of this work.

The setting up of a schoolteacher's camera angle reflects our belief that the seikatsu movement has something truly significant to offer teachers outside of Japan. Details, methods, theories, and philosophical bases of seikatsu writing education will be described throughout this book with the perspective of one who is interested in their application to writing education in the West. The Japanese experience is long-standing and well-documented. It represents an incredible reservoir of ideas and ideals on writing education already put into action and thoroughly tested in the Japanese context. It provides an opportunity to study writing education in a country where primary-grade student writing is a forte in many elementary schools. Specifically, the seikatsu curriculum provides a wealth of experience on process-oriented, writer-biased writing education designed to promote the cognitive and personal development of children. While seikatsu is not a direct counterpart of the whole-language philosophy or the process approach to writing, there are many parallels that make enthusiasts of those approaches compatriots to seikatsu proponents in Japan.

The book is organized into four main subdivisions. After the introduction in Part I, the philosophical tenets and historical background of seikatsu tsuzurikata are presented in Part II. Part III deals with topics related to teacher-student interaction, and Part IV with the seikatsu curriculum. Writer-biased approaches such as seikatsu tsuzurikata are considered in larger educational contexts in Part V. A concluding essay on the international implications of the seikatsu philosophy constitutes Part VI.

There are some points our readers need to know about the Japanese language. The suffixes *san, chan,* and *kun* are used with names (for example, Naomi-chan) as a sign of respect or affection. Generally, *san* is used for an older child or adult, *chan* for a girl or very young boy, and *kun* for a boy as well as for an adult male in certain contexts. These suffixes are commonly attached to first names of younger children and, as children grow older, to the last name, which usually becomes the term of address or reference outside of the family.

Japanese syllables are generally made up of a consonant and vowel sequence, or a vowel alone. Vowels are pronounced similarly to those in Spanish: *tsuzurikata*, for example, is pronounced approximately 'TSOO-ZOO-REE-KAH-TAH.'

Children's compositions were translated into comparable English as much as possible. When slang appeared in the Japanese version, we tried to find an equivalent English expression common to a child of approximately the same age in the United States. We tried to retain the tone and maturity level of the compositions, and the translations are as direct as we could make them. Errors that we found in the Japanese compositions were translated into equivalent errors in English. For example, a poorly punctuated sentence in Japanese was translated with a similar error in English. Wherever the Japanese students indented for a new paragraph, we made the same indentations in our translations.

ACKNOWLEDGMENTS

We owe an immense debt of gratitude to our own models of what it means to engage in seikatsu tsuzurikata education. Drs. Ken and Yetta Goodman of the University of Arizona nurtured this research from its inception with a seikatsu-like bias toward us as self-discovering writers. The Japanese educational philosophy described in this book was new to them, but they promoted our project by being ever ready with a scaffolding response to each forward and backward step that we took. There were more than a few times when they helped us pick up shattered pieces that we were tempted to abandon where they lay.

Ken and Yetta introduced us first to our primary contact in Japan, Dr. Michio Namekawa, whose guidance led us to the story of seikatsu tsuzurikata. His patient responses to our endless questions also modeled for us essential qualities of the methodology. Dr. Namekawa always seemed to answer exactly the questions we were ripe to have answered. Whenever we were able to articulate a new dimension of inquiry, he would smile as if he had been awaiting that event, then open to us a wealth of new data. As we read of his own pedagogical achievements, we realized that he was, as well, demonstrating the philosophy of seikatsu tsuzurikata. It hit home with us from these experiences that the whole-language movement and seikatsu tsuzurikata have in common an appreciation of the learner as leader.

Dr. Yoogo Shima of Tooyoo University spent many hours with the emerging theses of this manuscript, reacting to our ideas from his own base of study of the seikatsu tsuzurikata movement.

Teachers who invited us into their classrooms and circle-group meetings provided the vitality of the research process. We are deeply grateful to the many teachers who allowed us to disturb their classes, question their procedures, and dissect their collegial exchanges. Those who shared their professional lives with us are too numerous to list completely here. A representative sample must include Goro Kamemura, a remarkable teacher-author whose first graders demonstrated seikatsu education and from whose books and discussion sessions we borrowed extensively; Masao Hino, a most enthusiastic and insightful teacher-researcher, who opened his fifth grade to our note-taking gazes and then explained patiently the rationale for what we observed; and Hiroko

Iwatani, who is the epitome of the seikatsu teacher-colleague in her persistent probing for the best way to educate children.

Much of our research centered around the Chiba area just east of Tokyo where, in addition to others, we were welcomed into classrooms and meetings by Isamu Ariki, Kazuo Takeda, Hideo Kimura, Toshiko Yoshida, Yoshiyasu Ichikawa, and Takayuki Okamura, as well as Hatsue Ohgoshi, Chiyoko Hirakawa, and Yuuko Yamazaki. We would like to thank also the teacher-leaders of Tokyo Sakubun Kyooiku Kyoogikai (the Tokyo Writing Education Conference) who welcomed us into their meetings, and Tatsuo Ohtsuka and Masahiro Kusaki of the publication office of Nihon Sakubun no Kai (Japan Composition Association). We are grateful to have been able to learn firsthand about seikatsu from "annotated" visits to many other classes, such as Eiko Kouda's, Murao Yoneyama's, Hisakichi Kiriyama's, Noriko Niwa's, and Yoshiyuki Yoshimura's. Many teachers also shared their class anthologies with us.

Scholars such as Eikichi Kurasawa and Yukihiro Kawaguchi provided us with historical and philosophical dimensions that we would not have discerned without their aid.

We experienced the seikatsu writer's joy when James Britton responded to a draft of the manuscript with the nurturing specificity of the akapen or, as he would call it, the response of one who reads as a trusted friend.

Dr. Helen Slaughter read an early draft and contributed her insightful comments to the subsequent revisions of this text. And Rene Galindo gave us useful feedback after trying out some of the seikatsu ideas in his bilingual, first–second grade classroom. We thank both of them for their generous support.

Finally, we want to record here our good fortune in having had the opportunity to meet and work with Ichitaro Kokubun, whose death in 1985 marked the end of a long career as mentor and spokesperson for the seikatsu tsuzurikata movement. He realized the international importance of seikatsu tsuzurikata. We hope that we have contributed to that importance in our own small way.

INTRODUCTION

CHAPTER 1 — OUR RESEARCH BASE

Seikatsu tsuzurikata is a learning-through-writing philosophy that promotes self-awareness by having children select as topics something from their own daily lives. The extension from the self as topic and from the teacher (and classmates) as audience is deliberately paced slowly, so that children solidify their own position in the world before attempting more distant projections.

For us, an American elementary-school teacher and a professor specializing in Japanese linguistics, the compositions themselves attracted our attention first. We became intrigued with the expressive qualities of some of the compositions we happened to read and began to subscribe to one of the journals of this movement. We read such simple, direct compositions as the one by a first-grade boy from which this excerpt was taken:

TAKING A BATH

In the morning on New Year's Day my older sister woke me up and said, "Hiroyuki, take a bath."

I took a bath. The bath water was very clean and I could see my tummy and my legs. So I was in the bath for one hour and a half. The reason I stayed for one hour is that I wanted to clean myself.

The glass window in the door to the bath was different from usual and I thought it was peculiar. The pattern on the glass was reflecting light like flowers that I had never seen. I splashed some water and the flower petals disappeared right away. Because I was in the bath for such a long time, I felt dizzy. I drank three swallows of cool water and I felt better.

I told my family, "There are flowers on the glass." Grandma said, "Really?" Older sister Kazumi said, "Aren't they frost flowers?" And I said, "Oh, now I see. They were frost flowers."

About four o'clock in the evening I took a bath again. The frost flowers were still there and I thought they were pretty. . . .[1]

Mary made comparisons with some of her American students' stories, especially the ones she calls "stock-in-trade UFO and monster plots." She wondered how this child was able to write his simple observations with such straightforwardness. She was puzzled about the educational process that led him to consider this small perception as a topic for a composition. What difference made seikatsu themes such as the pulling up of a spring flower or the tasting of homegrown figs seem too mundane to compete in her students' minds with the retelling of last night's superhero story from television? And, if her students did write about such daily events, would their compositions contain elements of natural voice such as this one?

We examined various compositions and searched for answers to our questions by reading teachers' journal articles from Japan about this method. How did teacher-student interaction affect the students' voice? Which features might seem more speechlike, and what does it indicate when children slip speech patterns into their writing? How does reader awareness influence these children when the primary reader is the teacher? Mary began to take courses in graduate school to learn more about language and learning and experimented with similar writing tasks for her own students. We concluded that studying the development of writing by Japanese elementary-school children would interest both a teacher and a linguist. With the financial backing of a Fulbright-Hayes grant, we embarked on a seven-month study of seikatsu education in elementary schools of the Greater Tokyo area with side trips to other parts of Japan, including visits to some junior and senior high schools. Although this method of teaching composition is meant to extend into college, we concentrated our study in elementary schools because the higher-education aspects are less cohesively organized and relatively undocumented at present.

We began our observations in January 1984, which turned out to be a felicitous choice of month. Teachers were beginning their third and final term of the school year so they had good working relationships with their students, yet it was not as hectic as March, when the Japanese school year ends.

To establish for ourselves a clear picture of the implementation of the standards of the Ministry of Education, which both prepares and supervises the official national curriculum in Japan, we started by visiting teachers who do not consider themselves to be part of the seikatsu movement. In a Tokyo suburb we spent two and a half weeks visiting the classes of three teachers who were recognized as being avid about teaching composition, but not in the seikatsu tradition. There are variables, of course, between any two teachers or lessons, but the observations we made in the classrooms of these first-, third-, and sixth-grade teachers proved to be important because we could compare those well-taught lessons with the seikatsu lessons, also well-taught, which we subsequently observed.

Throughout February and into early March, contacts led us from one school to another. We visited a variety of seikatsu classrooms to observe composition education in action. And, even in the hiatus of early spring, before we felt we could again visit classrooms in the new term, which began in April, there were support-group meetings and national committee meetings of teachers who were willing to include us in their discussions. We found a wealth of written material in Japanese, because books and journals on the topic abound, most of them written by classroom teachers. Educators shared their class anthologies with us when they passed them out to colleagues in area meetings. Nevertheless, the heart of our research was the visits we made to the classes combined with the interviews we conducted with the teachers, for a process-oriented educational system cannot be studied from afar (through reading about it) or from the results (through studying its products); the activities themselves must also be considered.

To get into classrooms in Japan, one must have patience and a great capacity for green tea. There is no way to avoid the consumption of numerous cups of tea and delicious little sweets; they are necessary preliminaries to classroom visitations. Although teachers regularly open their classrooms on model teaching days to parents and colleagues, the general attitude is not to put students and teachers on display without first establishing rapport between the visitors and those being visited. The principal in Japan is a primary buffer between the school and the rest of the world. Many of the day-to-day problems with which American principals must occupy themselves are handled in Japan by the vice-principal, while the principal remains in a spacious, comfortable office awaiting occasions to officiate. When criticism is leveled against a school, as, for example, when a student has committed a theft in the neighborhood or has been hurt in a traffic accident, it is the principal who carries the heaviest burden (the Japanese school is expected to shoulder responsibility for lack of adequate guidance). But, when things are running smoothly, the principalship is often a good place to await retirement. For many, the role of principal is somewhat removed from the excitement of educational reform and innovation. Since these principals usually are not eager to have visitors who will disturb whatever tranquillity the school may have attained, calling attention, even of a positive sort, to individual teachers may be seen as a considerable request. There must be proper introductions, examination of credentials, and establishment of commonalities before the classroom doors will open. It was by passing this "principal barrier" that we realized how much of a grass-roots movement seikatsu remains after more than fifty years of existence. Administrators varied in their reactions, but generally they seemed either to be amused or confounded by our interest. In contrast, the seikatsu teachers themselves seemed to be functioning as proselytizers of the faith or guardians of the cause.

Seikatsu proponents maintain that this education is basic to cognitive and social development as well as a means of teaching composition. Historically, the methods emerged first in poverty pockets in Japan when teachers despaired of making relevant connections between some of the objectives of the national education system and the desperate living conditions of their students. Now its advocates promote it for children from all walks of life, but it remains a grass-roots movement that thrives because of the zeal of the teachers who believe in it.

The number of avowed seikatsu practitioners is difficult to gauge, and is likely to be rather small in any case. Its influence, however, is recognized even by its detractors, according to Eikichi Kurasawa, a past president of the Japan Reading Association. The movement flourishes, and has survived a turbulent period in Japanese history, as a teacher-to-teacher movement.

When written in Japanese ideograph script, two characters form each word of the term *seikatsu tsuzurikata. Seikatsu* is a compound of the characters for 'life' and 'energy,' meaning life as it is lived in the daily passage of time (i.e., 'life experience'). *Tsuzurikata* is made up of the characters for 'spelling out' and 'way.' Instead of reading *tsuzuri* as 'spelling out,' it can be read with the meaning 'binding' or 'patching together,' the fundamental meaning being that of making a connection, whether in writing or with thread.

Writing education in Japan today is usually referred to as *sakubun* (composition) education. Purists of the seikatsu tsuzurikata movement, however, favor the term *tsuzurikata* because it indicates the act of making connections with reality. The heart of the movement is the image of a child pouring some bit of his everyday life onto paper and, by doing so, realizing greater cohesion between himself and the world beyond. To the late Ichitaro Kokubun, a leader of the movement until his death in 1985, the image of a brush dancing down the page is symbolic of the word *tsuzurikata,* a "way of connecting," but the word *sakubun* is empty of such symbolism (1952:13; cf. Namekawa 1977:22–26 and Otobe 1982:98).

In terms of the process/product dichotomy so often discussed in the West by language-arts specialists recently, this philosophy and method represent a process orientation. Even though numerous anthologies of seikatsu-oriented writings of children have been published over the years, some making best-seller lists and even being made into popular movies,[2] it is not the products themselves, but the effect upon the writer that is the essence of seikatsu tsuzurikata.

We make no apology for the scarcity of statistical data in the text of this book. Such a study simply would not fit the topic yet. Instead we extended what Yetta Goodman calls "kidwatching" to include the teachers' interaction with the students (Y. Goodman 1978). Chisato's first return to a Japanese elementary-school classroom brought back a flood of memories and associations from his own childhood. After the first hour he complained, "Oh, it's so boring. I'll never be able to stand this." Then, as we discussed what had occurred from our varying perspectives, he began to take on that "kidwatcher" vision. It was amazing how quickly his enthusiasm for the actual classroom observations began to grow.

As the following diary entry by a first grader (which her teacher shared with us the next day) indicates, "visitor watching" has its appeal as well:

February 16.

Today Teacher Mary of America came to our school. She came for our language arts class. Although I had pictured her to be a prettier older-sister, she was not an older-sister but a mother. I was very happy to be seen by Teacher Mary. I was really happy because an American teacher came only to First Grade East Class. I'm glad she did not go to First Grade West Class. My heart pounded because Teacher Mary was watching us from the back of the room. I wanted to see what Teacher Mary was doing. I ended up turning around and looking at her.

She was with us for lunch. She ate the school lunch as if she enjoyed it. I was very happy, because if she was happy she might come every day. It'll be nice if she comes again.[3]

THE SEIKATSU MOVEMENT, PHILOSOPHY, AND HISTORICAL BACKGROUND

CHAPTER

WRITER-BIASED
WRITING EDUCATION

Writer-Biased Prose

"I saw an earthworm the earthworm Suzuki grabbed the earthworm"[1]
When her teacher saw this first grader's composition, he rejoiced.
Goro Kamemura wrote of his reaction (1980:19):

*I understood this composition because I happened to have been
there and to have seen her face at the time of the event, but if I
were not, I would still want to read into it and appreciate the mind
of the child which she wants to express through the writing.*

To Kamemura, the use of the word *earthworm* three times in quick
succession was not redundancy, but an expression of awe. The merits
of seikatsu tsuzurikata rest upon the teacher's role as a reader who
can tell the difference between redundancy and awe.

"I saw the earthworm the earthworm Suzuki grabbed the earthworm"
is writing with a stronger writer orientation than most readers will
tolerate. Such writing, however, is not limited to first graders. A self-
addressed memo—"Suit cleaners   Boy Scouts"—may give the rest
of the family information far beyond the words themselves. Although
a general audience gets little from this message, the family may be
able to make predictions about the writer's time of return, frame of
mind, dinner preference, or even weekend plans.

In both instances the writer has used words self-centeredly. The
words convey meaning only to readers who have familiarity with the
context and the writer. Such writing is writer-biased, not reader-biased.
Linda Flower (1979) and other researchers in the West have considered
the dichotomy between language functions that are strongly oriented
toward the writer and those that have greater reader consideration.
The distinction has been variously termed and described; our use of
the term *writer-biased*, extending from Flower's term, *writer-based*,
incorporates both the extent to which writer priorities overshadow
communication during the writing process and its application to pedagogy.
In the seikatsu classroom, writer-biased prose is not the teacher's

despair, not an evil to be overcome, but rather an indication of real self-expression. It is the writer, not the product, that the writing process nurtures. The philosophy focuses on an outcome defined in terms of beneficial effects upon the writer-self more than the text-producing capabilities of a potential author.

The first grader's experience with the earthworm was dramatic enough to inspire writing without much concern for audience. She used phrasing that she might blurt out to her mother upon her return home from school. She would not first consider her mother's need to know about the nature walk or who Suzuki is. We could modify the term "egocentric speech" from Vygotsky and Piaget and call her writing "egocentric prose." Britton calls it "expressive writing," and describes it as writing that remains "close to the self."

The first grader's writing served primarily to anchor the experience for herself by means of language. Preschoolers whose caretakers are sensitive to this aspect of development instinctively allow and encourage such anchoring in speech, just as seikatsu teachers do at school.

The earthworm watcher's teacher would model his response after the reaction the child's mother was likely to have. Not all listeners would receive the news by supporting what the child uttered before eliciting what is unclear about the communication. The way a parent typically nurtures expression without jeopardizing the child's confidence is the prototype of the way a seikatsu teacher nurtures writing. "You were really amazed at that earthworm, weren't you? And Suzuki grabbed it!" Such a response neither adds to the child's perception nor evaluates the child's language. It simply supports the expression that occurred.

Bruner (1975) used the term *scaffolding* to describe interaction that nurtures and builds upon the communicative process, and Graves (1983) advocates that teachers adopt similarly supportive strategies. Seikatsu writing teachers bolster the student's written expression by means of a written scaffolding response. Such support, whether by a parent in conversation or by a teacher in a seikatsu sort of response, adds an extra element to the discourse: it celebrates the fact that the child is using language. Adults provide each other with various amounts of such support, but only in special circumstances do we consciously nurture the talk of another adult. It is with children, for whom we assume a caretaker function, that we most deliberately apply supportive systems to receive and promote language. One way we do this is by utilizing the child's lead in our response, remaining somewhat neutral, if necessary, until the child's direction is clear. In other words, we delay imposing our own agenda on a conversation with a young child much more than we do with most adults. The seikatsu commentary on a child's writing similarly follows the child's lead and matches the child's mood. Here is an example of a beginning first grader's writing and the response of the teacher, Sadayuki Tanaka:

Teacher by the way there was a tomato a little red there was a small tomato too a little bigger one too hurry up gr-r-row you tomatoes.

[Tanaka:] Seeing those tomatoes, you want them to grow quickly so you spoke right up to them.[2]

And a further example:

Yesterday I was swordfighting with Kobayashi-kun. At Kensuke's turn he got me.

[Tanaka:] Namu myoo hoo renge kyoo [*I beseech you, great and wondrous in the power of the sutra*], namu myoo hoo renge kyoo; *Let Isono-kun's soul go to heaven;* namu myoo hoo renge kyoo, namu myoo hoo renge kyoo.[3]

Tanaka, in this second example, is going along with the mock swordfighting spirit and using a familiar Buddhist invocation as a funeral prayer.

Often, especially when teachers are working with beginning writers, the seikatsu teacher-child exchanges on paper are very speechlike, in keeping with the expressive mode. Writer-biased prose reflects the writer's domain and often has elements of speech as if it were not meant to go farther from the writer than speech goes from the speaker. Britton isolates expressive writing from that which has greater communicative purposes, such as "transactional," in which the writer attempts to involve the reader in some specific way like persuading or educating, and "poetic," in which the reader is presented with a holistically complete product as an artifact (see Britton 1975a, for example).

When teachers and other caretakers encourage writer-biased prose and ground students by appreciating that sort of writing, and only then make the most gradual extensions away from the writer, the selfhood of the writer is more likely to remain intact, even when the reader's needs become more and more prominent. That is the theory of Britton and others who advocate more expressive writing for students. In terms of the future benefits that will accrue to the writer's ability, Britton says, "Expressive writing provides an essential starting point because it is language close to the self of the writer, and progress towards the transactional should be gradual enough to ensure that 'the self,' though hidden, is still there" (Britton 1975b:15). The seikatsu approach, developed independently of Britton's wisdom, has a great deal in common with his philosophy.

To Read Writer-Biased Prose

The seikatsu curriculum begins with children writing in expressive prose. Their topics are their direct experiences. Helping them make a strong connection to reality is more important than teaching them to persuade, influence, entertain, or impress a reader. To accomplish this, the readership is controlled by the teacher, just as a parent tends to act as a buffer for the toddler's speech audience so that expressive qualities are preserved during development. Teachers exert this control by interjecting themselves as readers who are so empathetic that redundancy, gaps in information, and lack of conventional punctuation do not distract them from the writer's desire to share an experience.

The dialogue between the writer and her own personal reader is critical to nurturing cognitive and expressive progress. The teachers' special writer-aware response has the effect of reinforcing children who are getting used to the loneliness of communicating to a nonpresent audience. Beside a particularly descriptive sentence the teacher might write, "Wow, you are really remembering well, aren't you?" or beside an amusing part, "Toshi-kun, here you made me laugh so hard!" In the first of these, the teacher enters the time frame of the writing act as if he were looking over the writer's shoulder: "Here you are . . ." Using the present progressive and speech patterns such as the interjection "Wow" and the tag question "aren't you?" the teacher places himself into a position of immediacy with the writer at the time of the writing (cf. Kitagawa 1982). The second of these responses, "Toshi-kun, here you made me laugh so hard!" admits to a time and space separation that does not exist in face-to-face speech, but the teacher uses the child's name to help span the gap. The teacher's response is so critical that Kamemura has devoted an entire book to sharing his ideas on the best sort of "writing back" that a teacher can do (see Kamemura 1979).

When children write from top to bottom, as is typical in Japanese, the immediate margins are above and below the writing. Some teachers use one margin for more "literary" reactions and the other to respond emotionally to the content. Most teachers, however, mix their responses by simply writing spontaneously as they read. By doing so they hope to convey a natural, ongoing co-spectatorship with the child, as the following journal excerpt shows:

May 31, Tuesday, cloudy

"Yukari, they came up, they came up."   *A nice beginning. It is*
The moment I got home, Mom rushed out.   *clear she had news.*
"What came up?" I asked with my backpack   *I'd like to know too.*
still on.
My mother took me and opened the
kitchen door. Sprouts of kaiwari daikon
[*salad plants*] *we got from Grandma last*
night were coming up. I was surprised at   *What occurred is*
that since we just planted them last night.   *clearly written.*
My mother said enthusiastically, "It's great
fun. I wanted to show them to you right away.   *It's good that you did*
Real small seeds, but they certainly were alive   *not fail to hear this.*
after all."
The seeds were lying there split open and   *You are observing well*
from inside something like horns were visible.   *and in detail . . .*
The color of the buds was cream, like
bean sprouts. and with them there were tiny,
tiny things which looked like leaves. . . . [4]

Back in 1972 Britton described as an "unorthodox view" of the role of the teacher his recommendation that "the teacher needs to extend to the child a stable audience . . . a good listener, a good reader" (Britton 1972:37). It is essential for this third-grade journal writer's development to know on an almost line-by-line basis that her sending has been received. Writer bias does not eliminate reader importance; the act of writing usually presumes a reader, even when the writer is just writing for herself. Writer-biased readers, however, react to more than the words alone. The words are significant as evidence of the writing act. Writer-biased readers, then, are those who go behind the scene to find the author who waits in the wings. That is the element of celebration that connects to the support system children know in conversations with adults.

Less than three months after entering first grade, Sanae wrote about sunflower leaves:

Say Teacher the sunflower leaves are so big I could wear one for a hat. I want Akiko to wear one too.[5]

Her teacher took a cue from her writing and reflected it back to her with these words:

Sanae, what a good friend. When you thought of the hat, you wanted one for Akiko too. Since the leaves are so big, I imagine there are many things they could be.

Much of the writer-biased reader role that process-oriented teachers in the West provide during writing workshops in their classrooms is provided by the seikatsu teacher in these commentaries along the margins of journals and compositions. With as many as forty-five students in a class, these comments allow the Japanese teacher to reach every student on an almost line-by-line basis on every bit of writing.

The teacher can also use marginal comments to play the reader who is confused, who gently nudges the writer to be more generous with details or more logical in organization. "Hmmm. I wonder how those strawberries tasted." "Oh, now I see what you meant in the beginning part about the gate." Thus, while the reader role is evident, it is a known reader, a "trusted friend" (in Britton's terms) with immediate accessibility, and not a generalized, unspecified somebody, who might even read "as examiner" (see Britton 1975a).

"If That's What Writing Is, I Can Do It"

On one of the days of our visit to Kamemura's class, he happened to have a bit of spare time while most of the children were cleaning the room (as is the daily custom in all Japanese schools). He picked up a journal just turned in and called Emiko, the author, over to him. He put his left arm around the girl and began reading her journal entry aloud. Then, as she watched, he responded by writing comments in the margin, reading them aloud as he wrote. With more than forty students in class, this opportunity for Emiko to directly witness her personal reader in active response could not be a regular event, but every journal entry is returned promptly (often the next day) with extensive commentary. Children eagerly open their journals to see what has been penned in.

The reliability and sensitivity of this interaction is perhaps the key that we went to Japan to find. Children express themselves as if to say, "Is this writing? Am I doing it?" That is a critical question. By the nature of the teacher's response, children are able to answer their own question. "Yes, that was writing. And, if that's what writing is, I can do it."

Writing Community

After themselves as readers, teachers add a readership that is but one step removed: the student's classmates. From that immediate audience, known to the writer and reacting in the writer's presence, the composition may go to another class in the same school. Then it may be published in a class anthology. This is a standard practice in seikatsu methodology and usually occurs for every child with at least one composition each year. Teachers regularly share their students' compositions with each other by means of discussions at circle-group meetings, publication in journal articles, and the personal exchanging of anthologies.

Because of this predictable, responsive audience (and other factors such as the phonetic nature of the basic writing system in Japan), the products of seikatsu-trained children quickly progress to a level that makes the compositions look reader-biased in their attention to detail and sequence. But the writing process and the writer's inner growth are valued above the composition as an artifact that can be judged without consideration for the writer. For this reason, entering their students' writing into contests is anathema to many proponents of this method. Typical seikatsu publications are anthologies and are seen as resources to share and study. Publication serves the process, not the other way around.

Readers can be rewarded by the writer's generosity with details and careful attention to organization. ("Write so that we all can understand how it was" is a commonly expressed injunction.) But the readership is not the sort of audience that requires impressing or entertaining. Its attention is assumed. It is an audience whose primary function is to break through the text barrier in order to appreciate the writer's perspective. That is, the reader is not to stop at appreciation of the product, but should strive to understand more about the writer's connection to experience, a perspective that happens to be accessible only through the text.

Often, even if the writer is physically present when a composition is discussed, she is not consulted during the bulk of the session. The text must therefore be detailed, logical, and complete. More than that, it must represent the writer faithfully. Just as Kamemura responded to Emiko's journal entry as if it were actually Emiko, even though he had his arm around her shoulder at the time, the class is encouraged to regard the text as a representation of the author during discussion. As children experience this, they learn to project themselves toward the time when the text will represent them to a wider readership.

The audience, in this context, takes on a co-spectator relationship with the experiencer-self that the writer chose to portray. In this sort of relationship, Britton (after D. W. Harding, a British psychologist) suggests that, "what is afoot is a traffic in values" in "social imaginary spectatorship" (1975a:80). The spectator role allows writers to take an onlooker stance toward their own experience. The co-spectator role allows readers to reflect on that view of the world without having to participate in it. Writing in the spectator role does not involve attempts to manipulate the reader, who is, in turn, free from the burden of having to operate on the basis of the written text. Children in the seikatsu classrooms we observed were unusually generous in granting full attention to individual writers and their compositions for entire lessons. This, however, would not be a surprise to Harding, who characterized social imaginary spectatorship as a "basic social satisfaction."

The Writer's Self-Discovery

There is a fine line between reading to appreciate a text and reading to appreciate the writer's connection-making that resulted in the text. In the latter case, the reader and product are secondary to the writing act; they serve the writing act rather than being served by it. It might be compared to studying a van Gogh landscape in order to understand what feelings van Gogh had about the countryside flowers. In that case we are assuming that the act of painting is a recording of van Gogh's process of self-discovery, which we can then appreciate. Seikatsu teachers place so much value upon writing for personal growth that they stake their after-school time upon the belief that the combination of student texts and writer-biased commentary will give students a mirror to see themselves both as experiencers of life and as writers.

Japanese education is traditionally a whole-class system of education, rather than an individualized one, but seikatsu teachers endeavor to present themselves to each individual child as personal readers. (This, we were sometimes told, may account for the relatively small number of teachers who take up the seikatsu crusade fully: it appears to be an overwhelming undertaking.)

Most children begin by writing to their teacher-reader. "Write what remains strong in your mind about a certain day, a certain time" is the way most teachers indicate that a specific personal event is a good topic. This is the primary task of beginning seikatsu writing. It is the process of the writer connecting the self as experiencer with the self as writer without much concern for a readership, if the teacher has succeeded in setting up so comfortable a climate in the classroom. The techniques by which this climate is to be achieved are spelled out by teachers in books and journals and are discussed in local circle-group meetings as well as in national conventions. We will be more specific about some of them in subsequent chapters.

Writer-Biased Prose and Reader-Biased Prose in Contrast

It should be kept in mind that the assumptions we have made about the writer's role and obligations, and about the reader's, are not usually conspicuous when one looks at the products themselves. Even in observing an individual lesson, there is much that seems to be straightforward composition education under any name or theory. "Writer-biased" and "reader-biased" are terms to depict polarities that become apparent on the curriculum level, and writer and reader biases merely represent attributes on a continuum between those polarities. Often the margin of difference between these attributes is slight, although the cumulative effects may be pervasive.

We should also note that teachers in Japan we talked to did not describe themselves in terms of writer bias. Our characterization of this quality was confirmed, however, by every seikatsu proponent we asked. To some extent they seemed reassured that we had understood their objectives by the way we defined the term. Yet it often seemed that they tended to take the idea of writer bias for granted. When we discussed our perception of that attribute in seikatsu lessons, some would turn the conversation to describe how purely Japanese the seikatsu philosophy is. Such depiction of an essentially Japanese quality of seikatsu tsuzurikata may partially reflect the fact that Japanese literary attitudes and reading education in general have a tradition which is less reader-oriented than ours in the West. For example, in literary criticism the Japanese reader's interest in the author's upbringing and personal life seems to be assumed to a greater degree than is the case here. Similarly, even non-seikatsu classrooms we visited also exhibited what we would call writer bias during many reading lessons. In the Japanese context, seikatsu teachers' writer bias may be merely an intensification of what seems to be a cultural trait as well.

The following chart is a compilation of many researchers' implications about writer-biased and reader-biased prose. All components of writer-biased prose are identifiable in seikatsu writing as well as in the idealism of the movement's proponents.

Writer-biased Prose	*Reader-biased Prose*
Sometimes contains aspects of language usually reserved for speech	Is composed of language that is considered "written style" except for reported speech
Is process-oriented	May be product-oriented
Is "expressive" writing in Britton's terminology	Is either "transactional" or "poetic" in Britton's terminology
Assumes audience knowledge or empathy about the writer, i.e., a reader open to the writer's perspective	Should be reader-effective without personal knowledge or empathy about the writer

Connects writer-self to experiencer-self by means of writer's representation	Connects reader to text by reader's representation of text
Is "successful" if it makes the above connection, but may also enable some readers to gain access to the connection as well	Is "successful" if reader is influenced, persuaded, informed, or entertained according to the writer's intention

Seikatsu as a curriculum is a writer-biased process by which children are encouraged to explore fully their own connections to reality through writing for a limited, direct, and attentive audience. The fact that the products of this process can be appreciated as if they were reader-biased prose reflects not so much the goals of the curriculum as the fact that children are pressed to write explicitly and can accomplish this because they have an earlier written access to the scope of their spoken language than have their English-speaking counterparts.

We will continue this discussion on the comparison between writer bias and reader bias in chapter 16.

CHAPTER **3**

THE HEART OF SEIKATSU WRITING EDUCATION

November 19, Saturday, sunny
  I was riding a bus on the way home from school and then I was waiting a long time to get to my stop. And then I was about to push the buzzer, but somebody else pushed it first. And I looked at his face and saw it was another student from this school. And then when I looked at his face more closely, it turned out to be my older brother.
  And then we got off and my brother gave me a push. And then as we walked along my brother kidded me.
  And then he teased me in a loud voice, "I love you." I thought, "Hey, Brother, saying things like I love you outside in a loud voice, aren't you ashamed of yourself?" For me, saying such a thing even in my mind is touching.[1]

Kamemura says he burst out laughing when he read this diary entry, imagining the serious face of the first-grade boy who had so carefully followed his instructions to "look carefully and write exactly as you saw it. . . . He didn't have to use a slow-motion camera, I thought. Surely, if it was his own brother on the bus, he would have recognized him at first glance" (Kamemura 1971:17–18).

Writing a seikatsu-style journal turns the writer's attention back to a specific event. As described in Flower (1979), such writing focuses the cognitive process on episodic memory more than on the analytic or semantic possibilities. The foundation of the seikatsu curriculum is writing based upon a strong memory, however mundane, that occurred at a certain (recent) time. Hiroyuki's bath (chapter 1) was a single strong, but unspectacular, memory. To Mary, this was significant, for she had become discouraged with journals written by her own students in America. She had abandoned the practice because the entries tended to be empty recitations of typical daily activities. They had seemed to promote in the students a kind of generic writing, which finally rendered both the students and the teacher numb with the monotony. Students logged their days without distinguishing the significant from the routine, or they balked at the task when there was nothing spectacular to report. Their all-inclusive entries were a sharp contrast from the highly-focused *making the routine different*

Kokoro

seikatsu accounts based upon single memories. Seikatsu teachers stress that subject matter for writing may be anything that makes a routine different, and therefore memorable, however small: a surprise that made you laugh, gasp, exclaim, notice something, get angry, cry out— these are the things that tend to remain in your memory, however unimpressive they might be to a reader. Strangely enough, when this advice is followed, the results are anything but unimpressive!

The child first looks through one day's events (or very recent ones) for the single memory that remains vivid in his heart or mind. (Interestingly, the Japanese word *kokoro* means either 'mind' or 'heart'.) The child taps into inner motivation in the process of determining which single event to describe out of all current recollections. Once the event is singled out, teachers encourage students to make a prodigious memory search in order to strengthen the connection to the event through writing all the emotions, sensory associations, and thinking that accompanied it. The fact that the event must have been real but may have been only a fleeting experience is crucial to the goals of seikatsu writing. It is the child-writer, not the teacher-reader or the classmatereaders, who determines what is a good subject for a journal entry; the one requirement is a sincere desire to express a real memory.

Although seikatsu teachers all over Japan cherish the image of the child's intense encounter with his own life, the linkage between the student-writer and the readers (teacher and sometimes classmates) is crucial to journal writing, which is itself crucial to seikatsu tsuzurikata. It is writer-biased education because of the nature of writing expected, but around the writing act is a network of interactions that may be defined in terms of language-arts development, personal growth, community building, or cognitive development.

Cognitive-Linguistic Development

One way to look at this central activity (i.e., journal writing) in the seikatsu movement is in terms of inner and outer speech. Some of the journal entries sound like transcriptions of a conversational opening, as, for instance, the following entry by a first grader:

Say, Teacher, you know, I've never left any of my school lunch. You know, the school lunches are delicious.[2]

"Sensei, ano ne" (''Say, Teacher'') has become something of a catchphrase because so many first graders unconsciously begin their journal entries with that greeting. There are some teachers who actively discourage such speech elements, even in journals, but the interpersonal attributes of this education actually foster inclusion of traces of oral dialogue. ''What do you think, Teacher?'' sometimes appears at the end of an entry in anticipation of the teacher's response. That response seems to be a critical factor in seikatsu writing. This dialogic nature of the writer-reader relationship puts such writing into a position near the speech end of the language spectrum, which ranges from inner speech to formal exposition.

L. S. Vygotsky (1962) positioned spoken language between two extremes, which he called "inner speech" and "written speech." He noted that inner speech—the inner language by which people direct their mental activity—develops in children secondarily to outer speech. Outer speech emerges as part of the child's socialization. As the child's thinking begins to mature, some egocentric aspects of speech, which preschoolers often verbalize aloud, turn inward and become the basis for inner speech. Thought and language are not synonymous. There is both preintellectual and nonintellectual speech and both prelinguistic and nonlinguistic thinking. Throughout our lives we are capable of nonverbal thought and nonintellectual verbalization. But, during development, as Vygotsky has it, language and thinking intertwine so that a person is capable, in a significant sense, of thinking by means of language.

Inner speech is described by Vygotsky as "condensed, abbreviated speech" and is widely separated from written speech in terms of both grammar and semantic structure. The change from "maximally compact inner speech to maximally detailed written speech requires what might be called deliberate semantics—deliberate structuring of the web of meaning" (p. 100). Viewed thus, it may be argued that activities such as journal writing can be expected to strengthen the developmental interrelationship between inner speech and socialization.

According to Toshio Nakauchi, a well-known researcher on the seikatsu movement, by making the nature of inner speech clear, Vygotsky's theory helps to identify "the significance of the seikatsu curriculum in school education, a significance that has hitherto been attributed solely to the domain of intuitive experience" (1982:75). He claims that the crucial contribution of the seikatsu movement is not so much that its proponents have discovered the world of inner speech independently, but that, in their effort to fasten it to reality, they "have anchored it at the core of the educational curriculum" (p. 77).

Among the many forms of language that come under the headings "outer speech" and "written speech," following Vygotsky and also Moffett (1967), monologues, dialogues, letters, and diaries are closer to the inner-speech end of the spectrum. Journal writing, as practiced in seikatsu writing methodology, has elements of all four of them. The journal entries are basically monologues, often directed to a teacher who answers, as in a dialogue or letter; but there is also the personal quality of a diary. Writing a journal entry turns the writer's attention back to the event; reading an entry with writer bias focuses attention upon the moment of insight, whether that insight occurred during the event or during the writing act. The reader (including the writer when rereading) becomes a "spectator" (to use Britton's terminology) of both the event and the writing act. If writing is seen as engaging in a dialogue with some "other self," then reading, or rereading one's own work, is witnessing that dialogue. It is like taking your thinking out and examining its components. No wonder people say, "I did not know what I thought until I saw what I had written." Seikatsu writing teachers appreciate that image as well.

Interpersonal Relationships

Reading a child's journal opens the teacher's awareness not only to the moment of the writing but also to the moment of the experience behind the writing. Some teachers report that reading the journals after school causes the child's face to swim before their eyes in a special way that makes journal reading and responding a favorite kind of teacher homework.

Since most classes in Japan have more than half again as many students as American classes, the effort to know each child as an individual is a major undertaking. Tamiya (1968:9) describes how he makes an exercise of this early in the school term: using the class roll after school, he focuses on one name at a time, recalling that child and envisioning all the details of appearance and activity that he can. Such a memory search prepares a teacher to read such student narratives as, "I saw the earthworm the earthworm Suzuki grabbed the earthworm."

Kamemura got to know a first grader named Noboru better by recalling an incident at school at the same time that he read an (unrelated) picture journal entry by the boy (Kamemura 1982:56–8). When he saw the entry for June 18, he saw that Noboru had drawn a picture of a boy sitting on the crossbar at the top of a swing set, holding an open umbrella. Nearby was a woman with a look of consternation. The story explained how Noboru had jumped using the umbrella as a parachute. "At that time my mother was surprised. I sighed with relief." Seeing the entry with its graphic illustration, Kamemura recalled how, a day or so earlier, Noboru had been squirting the water from the drinking fountain when another teacher told him to stop. However, Noboru had squirted it one more time, wetting that teacher in the process. "When I read this so Noboru-like picture journal, I could picture again his face at that time, and affection for the boy bubbled up in me" (p. 58). Just as Noboru revealed in his journal a tendency to learn by doing things for himself (to the occasional dismay of parents and teachers!), children's journal entries might reveal more about their approach to problem solving than a whole series of math exercises would.

If, at this point, it begins to sound as if too much is being claimed for the role and benefits of journal writing and reading, then we are conveying accurately the almost mystical expectations zealous seikatsu advocates seem to hold for it. Britton mentions satisfactions inherent in what he calls spectator role writing (the expressive and poetic modes), but warns that "any attempt to specify them [satisfactions] is in danger of sounding like evangelical nonsense"; yet he dares to be specific with the following description, which would undoubtedly gladden the hearts of the seikatsu writing teachers we met in Japan:

1. When a child writes autobiographically he offers his experiences as a basis for forming a relationship with the reader he has in mind, a relationship of mutual interest and trust. . . .
2. When a child writes in the spectator role, whether autobio-

A. *First graders making paper-bag masks.*

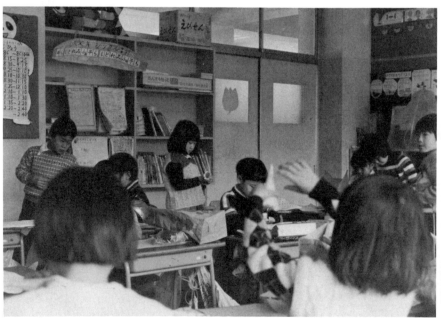

B. *Japanese schools accommodate six-year-old attention spans and energy levels.*

C. *Children dress warmly because schools are heated only on the coldest days.*

D. *Checking out the view from inside the masks.*

graphically or fiction, he exposes, by what he chooses to write about and the way he presents it, some part of his system of values, his feelings and beliefs about the world; and his satisfaction lies in having his evaluations corroborated, challenged, or modified. . . .

3. In offering his evaluations the child is in fact presenting himself in the light he would like to be seen in. Acceptance of what he offers confirms for him that picture. . . . Again, this is not an indiscriminate undertaking; it matters who plays the part of respondent.

4. There is finally the sheer satisfaction of bringing into existence a pleasing verbal object. . . . (Britton 1977:36–37)

The way in which one boy seemed to have internalized the idea of writing to form a relationship with the teacher as reader is implied in the following entry by a fourth-grade boy:

March 8, Sunday

It happened three days ago on Thursday. I was returning with Mogi-kun. On the train, Mogi-kun said, all of a sudden, "Maybe we should read the teacher's comments," and then he took his journal from his backpack. Thinking, "I want to take a look at Mogi-kun's journal," I said, "Hey, how about exchanging journals?" Mogi-kun thought for awhile and said "O.K." and handed me his. In return, I gave him mine. Both of us read intently for awhile. Truthfully, I was very surprised at the shortness of his journal entries. Mogi-kun went, "Hmmm" and said, "By the way, your journal entries are so long. Can't possibly be compared to mine. Don't you ever think about the teacher?" I thought, "What?" Thinking "What could he mean by that?" I asked him, "Not thinking about the teacher?" Mogi-kun said, "Sure. I'm writing very short things so the teacher won't get tired. But you write so long."

I don't think that's so. Although it might be too pushy of me and the teacher might get tired if we write long entries, the tiredness might go away if there is really something in it. On the other hand, if it's short and doesn't say much, the teacher might get more tired if he's disappointed. Mogi-kun might have forgotten this, but what he said made me think a lot. What do you think, Teacher?[3]

The journal is at the heart of all writing in the seikatsu writing movement because of the central purpose for doing it. Writing the journal taps energy in the child. Just as learning to speak is a basic drive upon which cognition builds, so also writing can become a natural extension of drawing and speaking, basic to inner growth. Therefore, both cognitive development and whole-person growth are nurtured. From a small pamphlet published by the Aomori Prefecture People's Education Research Center comes this explanation of the rationale for writing (quoted from *Ima, Kyooshi no Shigoto-o Mitsume-naoshite—* Now, to Re-examine the Teaching Task—in Shima 1984:101):

A child recognizes his own acts through language. He becomes aware of his thoughts and desires through language. He gazes at his other self and engages in dialogue with him through language. So therefore children must talk. And they must write.

We will discuss further the methods used to elicit such journal writing in chapter 8.

CHAPTER **4** LANGUAGE ARTS OR
SELF-ACTUALIZATION?

THE DAY GRANDPA CRIED

Itsuo said to my grandpa, "Masami's Grandpa, please tell us your impression." Grandpa finally said, "From Masami . . ." and his lips quivered. Everyone looked at my Grandpa's face. His eyes were red and he looked as though he was fighting to hold back his tears. The classroom became very quiet. Finally Grandpa said, "I am glad that I came to this year's Grandparents' Day." At that time the tears rolled down his cheeks. The old man next to him said, "It's a happy time." My grandma said, "So it is," and she looked at Grandpa's face. The old men and women there all clapped. I clapped too. After that, Grandpa was crying more. I saw Grandpa cry for the very first time.

I had been trying to persuade Grandpa from a week ago, but he wouldn't say yes. But I did not give up. Every year I would invite him to come to Grandparents' Day that we put on, but my Grandpa never came, saying "My work is busy." This is the last year that I attend this branch school so I wanted to make sure to have Grandpa come this year.

When Grandpa came back from work, I asked him, "Grandpa, please come to Grandparents' Day." But Grandpa just said, "Ummm," and then seemed to get lost in thought. He would not say he would come. A few days before the event my father, mother, Grandma, and even Older Brother joined the begging. Older Brother had never helped me in this sort of thing before. But he said strongly, "Why don't you go this year, Grandpa? This is the last year Masami attends the branch school. Next year, even if you wanted to go, you wouldn't be able to. Why don't you go for her?" I became happy. I never thought that Older Brother would say things like that, but even so, Grandpa did not say "I will go." I thought, "Oh, he won't go this year either." And I thought about the teacher. The teacher had been saying, as though he was really looking forward to it, "Masami, this year you must bring your Grandpa." I thought, "The teachers will really be disappointed." Then Grandma said, "Grandpa, let's go together." My heart began to pound and I thought this might do it. But Grandpa, smoking to-

bacco, still said, "You say that, but it will be embarrassing." I pulled his kimono sleeve and said, "Hey, Grandpa, please come." And I wondered why Grandpa doesn't understand how I feel. Then this time Mother said, "It will be really nice if you go with Grandma, the two of you together." Father said too, "If you go, everybody will be happy." I thought, "If he comes he'll enjoy it. But he does not understand that." I said, disappointed, "He says he isn't coming." Then Grandpa said, as though giving up, "OK, I'll go if you insist so much." I cried out, "We did it!" Everyone laughed. I made sure, "You'll come for sure." He said, "Um, um." And when I spoke again, "It starts at two, don't forget," he said, "Don't keep going on about it."

On Grandparents' Day Grandpa came, following Grandma. He looked lost when they got to the gate. I went to take him by the hand.

I saw Grandpa cry for the very first time, but he talked a lot with other old people too. I thought that he really enjoyed it. I thought that I should ask the teachers to invite him again next year also.[1]

This composition by a fourth-grade girl was discovered in a school anthology and was later presented in a panel discussion at the Thirty-Second Annual Conference on Writing Education in Kanazawa, Japan, in 1983. The title of the panel presentation was "What Is It That Has Become Important to Us?" It is considered to be an example of writing that represents a way of life from which others can learn. Such compositions are exchanged via circle groups and organizational publications.

The panelist, Shigeki Honma, first listed five points of excellence about the way Masami expressed herself: (1) the theme is clear and is carried out from beginning to end; (2) the organization begins with what impressed the writer, then goes back to explain the events leading up to that impressive moment, and concludes with her own desire; (3) descriptive qualities and word choices are excellent and reveal the careful way Masami observed; (4) she described also what went on in her own mind; and (5) dialogue was well remembered and expressed in a lively way.[2]

These points of praise represent the quality of written expression, or language-arts value, of the piece. Honma next pointed out that there could not have been such writing if there had not first been such character in the girl herself. The girl's strong motivation and persistence became the "prewriting" from which the composition could be written: "Without the qualities of the girl herself, this composition would not have been born." This is the self-actualization process for personhood that many seikatsu teachers feel is the essence of the curriculum.

A group of teachers, who are also circle-group leaders from around Tokyo, read and discussed "The Day Grandpa Cried," approving of Masami's persistence, which could be explored in class as a model attitude. Nonetheless, as later recorded in Nakajima (1984), a question was raised about the fundamental objective that teachers should hold for seikatsu training. Some argued that seikatsu teachers ought to zero in on the author's relationship with her family members without putting as much emphasis as Honma had on the literary quality of the composition itself.

One of the most persistent issues in the seikatsu philosophy concerns the definition of this type of education in terms of its ultimate objectives. A composite picture of the idealism we read and heard the most would be the image of a child who, through writing, becomes a whole person, grounded in reality, at one with mankind, nature, and society, and able to express selfhood through writing. Is seikatsu, then, language arts with self-actualizing benefits, or is it a self-actualization curriculum that teachers carry out by having children write? The answer is not readily available.

The process that results in seikatsu compositions constitutes a well-defined writing curriculum. The writing that students do in these class-rooms can be appreciated without regard for its implications for self-development. Indeed, there are many who would never want to fragment the philosophy into two streams. Dr. Michio Namekawa, a former seikatsu teacher, now a prominent author-professor in the field of education, has echoed this sentiment by describing these aspects of the philosophy as two sides of the same road.[3] A sizable number of seikatsu proponents, including many leaders, thus resist any prioritization that puts language arts ahead of personal growth. Is seikatsu language arts? Is it self-actualization? Perhaps the best answer is "yes."

The attitude that seikatsu tsuzurikata is more than language-arts teaching, that the child's personal development is in the hands of the teacher who engages in this form of education, gives the movement a spirit of holy mission. To some extent, many non-seikatsu Japanese teachers seem to share this spirit as well. Although there is also resistance to this image of mission out of concern that it may be used to hold teachers in a high status—low pay position in society, many Japanese teachers seem to take noncognitive education as a very serious responsibility, especially in elementary school.

Later in the meeting in which Masami's writing was discussed, the teacher-leaders considered another composition, which was presented by one of the members as a "problem case" from his own classroom. In it, a girl described a small physical deformity of hers which she felt was responsible for her ostracism by other students. She had first written about her unusual fingernail in the fifth grade and continued to write about it from time to time. Her teacher had hoped that the writing would begin to show some sense of resolution or insightful growth. Since the class had been together under the same teacher for two years, he hoped that, before she graduated from sixth grade, she would write in a less paranoiac way about her problem. He wanted to use the composition in class if the students were trustworthy enough; he did not, however, want to risk exposing her to insensitive responses from her classmates if they weren't. Had she written from a more stable perspective, the teacher would have felt comfortable with using her writing not only for her own benefit, but as a means of community strengthening within the classroom.

Some of the teacher-leaders argued against the extent of the teacher's caution in this regard, but the discussion ended with the conclusion by the group member who said, "The author's involvement in her own problem is too abstract, too detached. This issue is not whether to publicize this writing or not, but how to guide the girl to cope with the problem itself." As may be seen in these debates, personal-guidance objectives have a role in the seikatsu domain. This role has been constant in the tradition of the movement. Summarizing this particular day's discussion at the Tokyo circle-group leaders' workshop, the mentor of the group, a retired teacher, said, "I feel that this work described here today is like returning to the very starting point of seikatsu tsuzuri-kata. Expression technique is important, but children's lives are what we are concerned about to begin with."

CHAPTER COMMUNITY BUILDING AS
AN AIM OF SEIKATSU WRITING

I WANT TO LEARN TO MILK THE COWS

My main chores at home are preparing food for our cows and cleaning out the manure. Since I became a fifth grader, from about the end of May on, my work has increased.

It came about because, when Father was caring for the cows, one of the cows pushed him pinching his hand inside an iron device and injuring the ring finger on his right hand.

Because of that he cannot take the milk to the bulk cooler so that job is mine. . . .

The problem I have is that when I carry the bucket and try to put the milk in, I spill it quite often because the opening is so small.

When I say to Mother, "I can't help spilling when I pour the milk into the cooler," Mother says, "Oh, it's okay, because that's just a little bit. Don't worry. Pretty soon you'll be able to pour it in skillfully."

But I feel that I should not spill even a little bit. . . .[1]

When the copies of Kumiko's composition were first distributed, some of her classmates had moaned, "Oh, no, Kumi-chan has written about cows again." But it was a good-natured complaint; as their responses to the writing indicated, Kumiko's authority about life on a dairy farm was fully acknowledged. As for Kumiko the writer, she included in her elaboration about her work on the family dairy farm what might seem to be an unnecessary aside about her sister:

Mother almost always comes to do the milking, bringing my younger sister Wakako, when the work in the kitchen is done.

This is the same sister I wrote about in second grade when I said how happy I was that we were going to have a new baby. She is already two now.

This aside reflects the fact that Kumiko is writing specifically to an audience with which she has been sharing her writing for years.

Background

One of the goals of seikatsu education is "community building" or "class making." A rural area of central Japan known as Ena is particularly associated with the belief that the real purpose of education is to teach children how to live as people and what it means to be a member of society.

Ena is in a narrow valley without much arable farmland. This relatively poor area at the base of the Japan Alps has something of the same reputation as Missouri, America's "Show Me" state, in that its people are considered to be ruggedly independent. "Ena-type Education" came out of the disillusionment of postwar Japan, from which there developed a firm belief that education should be created locally rather than at the national level. The type of education sought by teachers and parents in the Ena region seeks to stress self-expression and societal awareness. One key factor in this education is a variation of seikatsu tsuzurikata that emphasizes trust building and interpersonal relationships among classmates.

Around the country also the term "class making" seems to be returning to the forefront in recent statements about the aims of seikatsu education. Independent strands of the seikatsu movement, such as Ena's, have come into the spotlight again.

Observations in a Fifth-Grade Class in Ena

The physical setting for our observation of a fifth-grade class in Ena was one of the most pleasant of our Japanese school visits. Misaka Elementary School is a warm-looking wooden structure, in contrast to the typical gray ferroconcrete schools found throughout Japan. Children walk to the school at Ena from as far away as eight kilometers, we were told. When they arrive, if they have brought their preschool siblings, they take them to the nursery school in the building. This is a service not usually found in public schools, an accommodation to a farming population in which the wife is often occupied with farm work because the farm income must be supplemented by the husband's taking another job.

All children go barefoot inside the school. Elsewhere in Japan schoolchildren remove outdoor shoes in exchange for slippers, but in this school it is felt that going barefoot is healthier. The floors have a rich patina, well-oiled by the caress of children's feet.

Noriko Niwa had also been the first- and second-grade teacher for the children she taught in fifth grade when we visited her class on a lovely day in late June. In this rural school she had only seventeen students. (Even though classes of thirty-eight to forty-five are standard in Japan, the Misaka School principal told us that he is allowed to avoid combination classes as long as grade levels have at least fifteen students.) Their desks were arranged in a U shape; we guests, including a class of fourth graders who also visited, were seated in the open end of the U.

Niwa explained to us the function of the small notebooks called "topic-searching books," that the children used. In them, students are asked to jot down potential topics about which they might like "to tell the teacher or classmates." Many, or even all, of these topics may never go beyond the listing stage. One of the trademarks of Ena's seikatsu education is the belief that students should never write because of coercion. They insist that such writing is not seikatsu tsuzurikata. The keeping of a list of potential topics, however, does seem to have a positive effect upon the child's willingness to write. It brings that subject, and whether or not to write about it, to the level of a conscious decision.

When the children are given journals in the beginning of the term, they sometimes complain loudly about not liking to write. Niwa says that she rejoices even over resistance about writing if it means that they are expressing real feelings, because that is the beginning of the self-assertion she wants to promote. When a student does write and submit a journal entry, she lets that student and the class know how important that is. Soon, without coercion, she says, most students do begin to write, and the complaining shifts to irritation whenever writing time is disrupted. Other Ena teachers told us that some students do resist writing completely and may not use their journal at all from year to year, but still such teachers refuse to resort to pressure tactics. They maintain that the basis for seikatsu tsuzurikata begins with an unpressured desire to write. The decision and the timing must be in the child's control for the writing to achieve the sort of impact upon the child and the classmates that the teachers anticipate. Such flexibility does not seem to prevail where seikatsu focuses more on language-arts education.

Four days before our visit Kumiko had written her piece on the subject of milking cows at home on her family's farm. Niwa had duplicated the piece and had given every student a copy to read at home the night before our visit.

Kumiko stood and read her composition aloud. In addition to writing about pouring milk into the bulk cooler, Kumiko wrote about trying to help out by "stripping" the udders of the cows after the milking machine was removed. To her disappointment, she reported, she really could not get the hang of it. When she told her father that she thought it was her lack of strength, he had said it was more a matter of skill.

The writing was actually not very well organized. This, we were told, is often the case in writing by these students. It may reflect the fact that language arts is not as high a priority as self-expression and the sharing of one's life in the group.

As we had seen in seikatsu classes elsewhere, Kumiko remained silent during the discussion, even when questions were raised that she could have answered spontaneously. As the following excerpt of the discussion illustrates, her writing was all that represented her to the class until she was given a turn to respond at the end, and even then she did not answer their specific questions (T = Niwa, the teacher; C = various classmates; K = Kumiko, the author of the piece):

T: Tell Kumi-chan anything you want to say.

C: You milk the cows so late in the evening? I thought that cows usually get milked in the afternoon. Don't the cows get sleepy?

C: When do dairy trucks come by to pick up the milk?

C: Aren't the milk buckets awfully heavy?

C: Why do you put medicine on the cow's udder after milking?

C: How did your father's hand get injured?

C: My home also used to be a place where we kept cows. My grandma used to help. If you can help so much when you're only in the fifth grade, I think that's great.

C: Why do cows get excited if it's noisy?

C: Your attitude toward work, now that you have even more to do since the accident—that's really a good spirit.

C: What if it rains into the milk when you're carrying a bucket?

C: Your father knows a lot about the skill of milking.

C: You have a good attitude toward your sister, too.

C: I didn't know that milking really took skill. I thought anyone could do it right away.

C: What is the bulk cooler like?

C: I understood well about the milking machine from your description. I didn't know what it was called before.

C: I think it's good that you are worried about wasting milk when it drips as you pour it into the cooler.

C: I'm impressed by your desire to take on even more work.

C: You do work hard.

C: I can only eat meat and drink milk, but Kumi-chan can do all these things for food production. . . .

T: Kumi-chan, what did you feel when your classmates talked about your writing?

K: I wanted to write again to add in their ideas and the answers to their questions.

T: Someone else please read Kumi-chan's composition. Read it as if you were Kumi-chan so she will be ready to write more.

We later asked Niwa to predict the effect of the classmates' comments on Kumiko's future writing. She said that, since the comments were not written down, she expected Kumiko to absorb only those that are important to her; that is what will appear in future writing.

At noon we watched as the entire student body performed local folk dances in the schoolyard to music over the public address system. It seemed to be a fairly regular practice in that school, and part of the community-building curriculum as well. The easy mingling of younger and older students and the un-self-consciousness exhibited by the students made it seem more like a celebration than a performance.

Community Building

As is true in Japanese society as a whole, the sense of group spirit, teamwork, and interdependence prevail in Japanese education. In a culture so embued with community concerns, what is the role of seikatsu education? We feel that it is actually an enrichment of the individual as a group member. In a highly individualistic society, an antidote to anarchy would be activities that promote cooperation and consensus. But in a society such as Japan's, where geographical, historical, economic, and traditional forces tend to elevate the group above the individual, seikatsu group making begins by stressing personal strength and self-awareness.

One year Niwa read a poem by a well-known seikatsu leader, Yoshio Tooi, to her class. They liked it so much that they made a paraphrased version and posted it on a chart to be read aloud by the group each day. Their version of the poem illustrates the relationship of individual to group, which Niwa describes as an objective of such community building.

I AM MY OWN HERO

I am the only I in the world.
I am the only one responsible for myself,
So I'm not going to despair over things difficult.
It's foolish to ruin myself with my own anger;
I'll persist even when it's not easy to go on.
I'm going to empower myself
Because I'm the one who owns me.
If it only matters to survive,
Well, even earthworms survive,
But I'm human so I want to live meaningfully.
If it only matters to struggle on,
Well, even caterpillars and centipedes struggle on
But I'm not a caterpillar or a centipede,
So why not concentrate on things that bring joy to others?
Even the earth revolves around the sun
As well as turning on its own axis.
Let's persist also in making a wonderful class
Let's persist also in creating a close community
By sharing one person's joy with everyone
And rejoicing for each other with a greater joy,
Sharing with everyone any individual sorrowing,
Bearing it together and making it smaller,
Driving out relationships of bullying and being bullied,
Driving out relationships of teasing and being teased.
Why not fill the world with light,
The world in which each individual light shines forth?
It's the community in which I live
And I am the one responsible for myself,
My own hero.

In her book, *Asu ni Mukatte* (Toward Tomorrow), Niwa describes the sort of advice by which she enjoins students to be individual members of a caring group (Niwa 1982:35):

Good writing is born of a very lively life. When you read a friend's writing you have the experience of getting mad with the writer, rejoicing with the writer, and you think, "Gee, I wish I could write like this." . . . How to write: (1) know what you want to do in life, then grapple to achieve it with all your power; (2) train your mind to use your eyes, ears, hands, feet, and mind anywhere, without overlooking anything, then be happy, angry, surprised, anxious, et cetera; (3) articulate clearly what you want to write; (4) remember precisely the circumstances of the time and the feelings, then write in detail as it happened, choosing the words carefully; (5) read your own and others' writings and discuss them together—grasp your own life surely and compare it thoughtfully to your friends' lives.

The issue of schoolchildren's privacy is not generally debated in Japan as it is in this country. Moral education is a mandated part of the national curriculum, and the teacher is given responsibility for the children's attitudes and behavior, even outside of school. Seikatsu teachers, however, do consider themselves to be responsible for each student's sensitivity and privacy. Every teacher we questioned on this matter had built some system of confidentiality into the seikatsu program.

In *Toward Tomorrow* Niwa describes how a student named Izumi wavered during all of fifth grade before deciding to write about a disabled aunt who lived at his home. He suffered from embarrassment over her actions when his friends visited, but had not really faced the reality of her existence and its effect upon his family until he chose to write about her in sixth grade. Niwa says that the essence of seikatsu is letting him be the only one to make the decision about whether or not to write about such a sensitive topic. As it was, he gave her many clues, each one less obtuse, that he had something he felt ambivalent about confronting. She particularly noticed that he was "beginning not to avert his eyes" when he wrote, "I do want to write, but I don't want to. I think when something is really difficult, one cannot write." Niwa waited. One day he came to school with seventeen pages he had written at home about his aunt. He approached Niwa privately and showed the writing to her, insisting, even against her hesitation, that it be shared in class. A trip to a special school for severely handicapped children had been scheduled, and Izumi said he wanted this piece to be used as a prelude to the visit. Niwa went to Izumi's home and had him read and discuss his writing with his family. After they agreed to it, she opened it to the class. Izumi described the experience of deciding to write this way (quoted in Niwa 1982:167):

When Miyuki read aloud her composition, she added tearfully, "I thought that you would understand, and so I wanted all of you to know. I thought first I wanted only the teacher to read it, but then when I trusted the teacher, I trusted you [the class] too." . . . That moment, I felt that I could write also. I felt that I could write about Hatchan honestly. Since then, I thought deeply about how to write it.

In the class-making aspects of seikatsu philosophy, there is an implied definition of community, which envisions a group of individuals who are unafraid to share their perceptions, thoughts, and feelings in the cause of greater mutual understanding. What such a community requires is, first, depth of study by individuals regarding their own contact with reality, and then the openness for this individual awareness to be shared with and received by the group.

CHAPTER **A HISTORICAL OUTLINE OF THE SEIKATSU MOVEMENT**

EARTHWORM

My grandma hates earthworms. When she sees earthworms she says, "Oh I hate it, hate it" and she runs away.

When I was pulling weeds there came out a gigantic earthworm so I got it on the tip of a stick and went inside calling out "It's an earthworm." Grandma was shocked and ran off. And she screamed at me, "You idiot. Don't come back home."

I called my younger brother and we cut up the earthworm and played house with it. Then we built the earthworm a tomb.

"Earthworm" (as quoted in Kawaguchi 1980:125) was written by a first grader in about 1930. It was said to be one of the favorite compositions of Tadayoshi Sasaoka (1897–1937), a highly influential, seikatsu-style teacher. Sasaoka's teaching, while he was still a beginning educator in a mountain village on the island of Shikoku during 1917–20, is considered by the education historian Toshio Nakauchi (1977, 1982) to represent a prototypical model of seikatsu education. As a teacher returning to the village where he had once lived as a youngster, Sasaoka found it deserted by most young people, a situation reflecting Japan's rising industrialization and the radical changes that accelerated from World War I on. The small mountain village was lifeless with only those who were either too old or too young to leave. Hardly anyone subscribed to newspapers. He felt that in this context the premise of the Ministry of Education's directives on modern education, built fundamentally on the children's ability to read in various fields of a compartmentalized curriculum, was utterly foreign and wrong. Whether consciously or unconsciously, he resorted to a premodern form of education that traditionally commoners had been used to, namely, an education based on writing to carry on the necessities of daily activities. Sasaoka molded his entire educational plan into what we would now call typical seikatsu writing. He saw in it a path where teacher and students can meet as active participants in a process that might make a real difference in children's lives. Seikatsu writing, then, was not just one of the subjects within a larger curriculum; it signified the whole education.

The view that seikatsu tsuzurikata has its roots in the premodern writing education for common people in Japan is expounded by Nakauchi (1977:27, 651, 762 and 1982:174–78; but see Taroora 1983) and supported by Shima (1984:178). As for premodern Japanese education itself, Dore (1965:124) comments on "the divorce" in the Tokugawa period (1603–1867) "between the teaching of writing (Japanese) and the teaching of reading (Chinese)"—"the reading of Japanese was not something that was specifically taught or practised; it was developed as a by-product of practice in writing" ("writing" in the functional sense; cf. Passin 1965:48).

In Nakauchi's view, what distinguishes the seikatsu movement from those which have also emphasized the importance of children writing about their lives rests in its adherence to premodern, agrarian human values—in defiance of the dehumanization implicit in state-dictated industrialization. It is in this light that he sees in Sasaoka's teaching activities a prototype seikatsu formula.

Except for this peculiarly Japanese qualification, Sasaoka's teaching was perhaps rather close to Dewey's ideal. Shunsuke Tsurumi (1956) characterizes the seikatsu movement as "Japanese pragmatism." Sasaoka as a teacher seems to have personified that spirit in many important respects. Although not an acknowledged Deweyan in any sense, he, like Dewey, strongly valued independence in a child. Compositions with the rather untamed vibrancy of "Earthworm," quoted above, were the type he often praised.

From 1930 to 1937 Sasaoka was an editor of the landmark seikatsu journal *Tsuzurikata Seikatsu* (Writing Life Experience) (1929–37). In the first issue under his editorship a policy declaration appeared with the first clear pronouncement about seikatsu tsuzurikata on a national scale:

(1) The ideal and method of real-life education is attained by observing clearly the real issues of society and actual facts of children's lives . . . and (2) tsuzurikata [connection-making writing] is the central discipline for real-life education.

The seikatsu movement is often traced further back, however, to a teacher who was never involved in the seikatsu movement himself. Yet Enosuke Ashida (1873–1951) paved the way for the emergence of seikatsu tsuzurikata by propagating the view that children should write naturally about themselves (Ashida 1913). This was a striking view at the time. The following anecdote, recorded in Namekawa (1977:174–75), graphically illustrates how revolutionary it was.

One of the popular magazines for children around 1890 in Japan was *Kooganshi* (Young People), which carried compositions written by its youthful readers. The editor of an 1891 issue noted that, of 57 compositions by elementary-school children on the topic of outings, 27 contained passages describing the author's indulgence in wine drinking and singing. This editor was moved to stress that by publishing those compositions the magazine was not encouraging children's drinking, but was accepting the fact that the young writers were following the long-standing literary convention that when one wrote about an outing, one wrote about drinking wine and reciting poems; what the children perceived to be at issue in writing those compositions was the mastery of literary convention, and not the telling of their own stories.

In this continuing ethos, Ashida's suggestion that to write tsuzurikata is to express oneself met with strenuous resistance. But it was in this that Ashida is generally considered to be a ground-breaking precursor of the seikatsu movement.

It is interesting to note that Ashida came to this idea through his encounter with Zen Buddhism. Disillusioned and burned out in his efforts to adhere to the curriculum directed by the Ministry of Education, he turned to a Zen counselor, Torajiro Okada, who would simply sit, talk, and meditate with him in an essentially nondirective counseling atmosphere. Ashida was to recall later that these *zazen* (Zen meditation) sessions with Okada were the turning point of his life: prior to that, he lived to meet the requirements of the external world and was exhausted; afterwards, he lived for the fulfillment of his inner self and was at peace. For Ashida, with his Zen orientation, all affairs of the external world were ultimately reduced to the state of selfhood. In this, his teaching was clearly distinct from that of seikatsu teachers, who were to focus more on their students' daily lives as a locus of a critical interconnection between two realities: their selfhood and the context of the society in which they lived.

Namekawa (1978:314) lists three theorists on children's writing as crucial contributors to the intellectual ethos from which the seikatsu movement emerged as a popular grass-roots movement of concerned teachers. One is Enosuke Ashida; the others are Shinkichi Tanoue (1889–1945) and Miekichi Suzuki (1882–1936). Tanoue was the first person in Japan to articulate the view that the purpose of writing education rests in children's self-actualization and in teachers' guiding children to express their life events. (The basic theoretical framework of Tanoue's position, reportedly, was Henri Bergson's (1859–1941) view of *l'énergie spirituelle*, which was exceedingly popular in Japan around 1920.) An instructional plan recorded in Tanoue's 1921 book *Seimei no Tsuzurikata Kyooju* (A Curriculum of Life Energy Writing) directed children to observe the special year-end sales as preparation for composition writing (quoted in Namekawa 1978:309). Instructing the children to carefully observe those things that might particularly characterize the occasion, he suggested: "Open your eyes, look at the shapes, movements, color, and light; open your ears, listen to sounds, voices, conversation; smell; feel, with the whole body, the chill, the cold. . . ." For actual writing, he instructed: "Recall the experience, look at the scene inwardly, and bring the scene in front of the eyes; write when your senses are full and the idea is jelled." What was important to Tanoue was an intuitive appreciation of one's own life; writing was important because it brought out that process. Some seikatsu teachers in the northeast region of Japan were to criticize his approach some years later as being too narrowly self-centered. But his proposal, when it was published, had an enormous impact on young leaders in writing education, including would-be seikatsu teachers across the nation (cf. Namekawa 1978:312, Sasai 1981:46).

Of the three people mentioned by Namekawa, Miekichi Suzuki (who is customarily referred to by his first name, Miekichi) was the only one who never was a teacher. He was already an established author when he started *Akai Tori* (The Red Bird) (1918–29, 1931–36), a famous monthly literary magazine for children. The magazine, designed to set a new standard of literary sophistication for young readers, boasted a host of well-known literary figures among its contributors. It also provided space for children's compositions, for which Miekichi gave children the following advice (as quoted in Namekawa 1978:175):

Please, whether long or short, submit your writings, which are not created by superfluous imagination, but written exactly as you saw it, as you heard it, and as you thought about it, in a natural manner. . . .

Write exactly as it was—this was a hallmark of the *Akai Tori* realism, and it was in this that Miekichi's proposal shared a common ground with seikatsu writing philosophy. This view of his undoubtedly was related to his view of literature. It was a time, as Ichitaro Kokubun (1982:25) was to recall, when such authors as Balzac, Stendahl, Dickens, Tolstoy, and Dostoevski had profound impact on the field of writing in Japan, each author's proponents claiming their own version of "realism" and "naturalism." What Miekichi brought to the field of writing education through *Akai Tori*, however, was his devotion to excellence in writing. The number of compositions submitted in the first year of publication was about 300 a month; it went up to about 2,000 a month in its fourth year (Namekawa 1978:178).

The composition from which the following excerpt is taken was entitled "Mother." It is an account of his mother's death written by a Hokkaido fourth grader, Michio Iida, and published in the March issue of *Akai Tori* in 1928 (as quoted in Nakauchi 1977:401–3):

I was about to go to school. Mother said to me, "Michio, skip your classes today." And she made me stay home. She said, "Look at my arm." And she lifted her bone-thin arm from under the covers. She was sleeping all that day. At night I swept the yard. Then I washed the pans. When the milk got warm, I took it to her. She was sleeping with her arm outside of the covers. I said, "Mom, here. I brought milk." She didn't reply. I said, "Mom, here." And I tried to shake her a little. But she kept her eyes closed. Her face was real pale. And she did not say anything. I was scared. I ran next door and got the next door lady to our house. She shook Mother, saying, "Say, what's happening?" Then she took off the covers and put her hand on Mother's body. And she said, "Michio, your mother is dead." I cried aloud. The next door lady said, "Don't cry, don't cry." She was crying and said, "Your poor Mother. She is so thin. She really cared about you so much, and

*she had to die." Then she prayed holding her palms together. I
went next to Mother. She looked so pale, her hair had grown long
and she looked asleep.*

Miekichi's approach to children's writing was radically different from
that of seikatsu teachers in one crucial respect. It was, as Nakauchi
(1977:396–405) and others point out, product oriented (i.e., reader-
biased). Nakauchi cites for this an example such as the following
comment by Miekichi (quoted in Nakauchi 1977:401–3; the emphasis
is Nakauchi's as well), which seems to focus more upon the writer's
literary accomplishment than the child himself:

*The description of the next-door neighbor touching the author's
mother's body to learn that she is dead* brings the scene vividly before our *eyes and evokes an unspeakable feeling of pity.*

What Miekichi was concerned about was the power of the writing.
What seikatsu teachers are concerned about are the lives of the young
people they deal with.

Seikatsu tsuzurikata was to spring from a turbulent period in modern
Japan. The worldwide depression in 1929 hit Japan with full force.
Problems in farming communities were compounded, particularly in
northeastern Japan, by unusually cold weather in 1931. A war in
Manchuria, in which Japan was deeply involved, also began in 1931.
Japan was hurtling toward militarism under the pressure of nationalism.
The Sino-Japanese War began in 1937, and Japan finally plunged
into World War II in 1941. It was a time of national convulsion dictated
by right-wing ideologies, in which the value of human existence was
measured solely in terms of its service to the national interest. It was
in this context that seikatsu teachers attempted to help children find
their own human values even against the spirit of the times. From the
late 1920s to the end of the 1930s, many compositions were written
under the guidance of those classroom teachers across Japan, particularly
in the northeast region, where financial straits were the most severe.
Most of these compositions—which were to be popularly referred to
in subsequent years as *seikatsu tsuzurikata*—articulated the authors'
actual lives, and the teachers had to cope with the descriptions of
hardship written in them. The seikatsu movement, as popularly conceived,
grew out of those teachers' desires to help their students, whose lives
contained little but despair. There arose the aim of encouraging the
kind of self-determinism that could not be overcome by hardship. As
Rokusuke Takahashi, a teacher in the northeastern region in the late
1920s, stated (quoted in Kawaguchi 1980:156):

*The root of her [the author of a composition Takahashi is com-
menting on] suffering clearly resides in poverty. . . . Education is
completely helpless in the face of this reality. But does that mean
that there is nothing we teachers can do? There must be something
we can do. What is it? A teacher can be a friend in the midst of*

*this adversity, appealing to her will to survive, strengthening that
will, and prodding her to go on to establish her own place here.*

Totalitarian suppression was coming, however. In 1940, and continuing after the declaration of World War II, a number of seikatsu teachers
were arrested by police on "anti-Japan activity" charges. Namekawa
(1983:513–14) reports that 135 teachers had been arrested by the
end of 1942; over ten of them died in circumstances attributable to
their prison experiences. The seikatsu movement was crushed. (There
are a number of publications on this governmental persecution of the
seikatsu movement in 1940–42, including Kokubun 1984c, which is
his personal account of the ordeal.)

World War II ended in 1945. The first groups that stirred excitement
in children's writing after the war were commercial publishers. A number
of magazines for children were published then, the most well-known
among them being *Aka Tombo* (The Red Dragonfly), which was launched
in 1946. It solicited compositions from children. The appeal to the
public in the first issue was as follows (as quoted in Ouchi 1984:22):

*Send us good compositions, everyone! Your writings are the eyes of
your heart. Through writing, you can see through your feelings, and
you can make your actions in daily life stand out clearly. During the
war you were forced to write only what you were supposed to
write. But now you will express yourself freely without any such
restraint. . . .*

The person in charge of selecting compositions for publication was
Yasunari Kawabata, who was to receive the Nobel Prize for Literature
in 1968. His comments for the occasion of the first issue included the
following (as quoted in Ouchi 1984:22):

*If even the spirit of children should become that of a small and
weak nation, we will surely become inferior people. I want to pre-
vent that, by contributing to the enhancement of children's writing. I
think that, perhaps, we should not look for too artistic writing or
writing of gifted children with special training. . . . I want also to
value writing by healthy average children. That is, I will try to maintain a standard attainable by every child. I want it to be known that
children can grow through writing and can more surely ascertain
their lives in their everyday settings.*

The year 1951 was an important year in postwar Japanese history.
The American occupation of Japan formally ended, and the United
States–Japan Peace Treaty was signed. It was also the year that three
exceedingly popular books associated with the seikatsu movement were
published. *Yamabiko Gakkoo* (Mountain Echo School), compiled by
Seikyoo Muchaku, was a collection of writings (personal narratives,
study reports on local community finances, and poems) by his 43
eighth-grade students in 1949–50 in a small mountain village in northeastern Japan. *Atarashii Tsuzurikata Kyooshitsu* (New Tsuzurikata

Classroom), written by Ichitaro Kokubun, was an introductory book on the theory and application of seikatsu tsuzurikata, both as it had been practiced before World War II, and as it was envisioned to be relevant in contemporary Japan. And *Yamaimo* (Mountain Tuber) was a collection of poems written by Matsusaburo Oozeki (a sixth grader when the poems were written in 1937–38) and compiled by his teacher Michio Sagawa for publication after Oozeki's death during World War II. These books made such a tremendous impression on the general public that seikatsu tsuzurikata became a household word at that time.

Yamabiko Gakkoo is particularly descriptive of the ethos of the time in which it was published. The students whose writings are represented in this book were the first Muchaku taught after his graduation from college in 1948. He stayed with them from the seventh through the ninth grades. Upon arriving at the school, he had found the village and the school in utter poverty and the academic level of the students dismally low. He set as his teaching goal the instilling in his students of a sense of human dignity and a relentless search for answers based upon facts. He explains, with biting humor, how the writings in the book came about (Muchaku 1969:257–59):

[*These writings*] *were due to our desire to get involved in real education. If we look, for example, at the Ministry of Education directed social studies textbook 4,* Life in Rural Japan, *which our students read, we come across the following statement: "A village normally has an elementary school and a middle school. The nine years covered by them are compulsory education. Therefore, each village builds these schools with proper facilities to provide good education for children in the village" (p. 10). I realized that, in teaching that passage literally, I would be a shameless liar. In reality, a village school like ours has no maps to study and no equipment to do any scientific experiments; education in our school is carried on by teachers who have nothing to depend on but a piece of chalk, in a dark classroom with a thatched roof, snowy winds blowing in through the torn paper screen windows during class. The village administration, beset by financial difficulties, has enough money to provide but a fraction of what the textbook describes as our standard facilities. What dawned upon me finally was the unfathomable wisdom of the Ministry of Education's claim that social studies was a discipline that could not be learned in a textbook. . . . I kicked myself for not having perceived this message before. And once I understood the irony, I could not just continue on as I had been. I thought and I agonized. And, finally, I came upon the idea of having my students write. . . . Compositions and poems in this book were all written as starting points rather than as end products. Each contains pertinent issues, and each was discussed in class carefully. . . .*

"The Low Land" is one such composition, which was actually also a social studies lesson:

"It'll be interesting if you find out how your family's farm or rice fields came to be the names by which they're called." I had just remembered the teacher's saying that so I asked, "Dad, why is our place called Kubo?" He answered me casually, "Because that's just what it is, a 'low land.'" I asked, "Well, then, how many tan [about a quarter-acre measurement] is Kubo farmland?" At that, Father suddenly looked stern and said, "You, don't you go investigating such things. You were trying to find out some such thing the other day too, saying it was for social studies. You are telling all this to your teacher, aren't you? The teacher is being asked to get this information by the prefecture office, so if he reports larger figures then we'll have lots of trouble. Things will go on until we won't be able to feed you. So you don't have to know things like that. When the teacher asks, just say 'I don't know.' And from now on don't ever ask such a thing."

When our teacher first came, he shouted from his platform at us, "To study is to think 'why?' It is not to memorize. It is to develop eyes and ears, the entire body, that says 'right' when something is right and 'deceit' when something is deceit. It is to nurture a soul that is strong enough to put this into action." One year has passed since then. All during this time the teacher would not let us forget this for a moment. In student government and on any other occasion he always makes us discuss this fully and keeps us thinking. Because of that, the spitwads, marbles and even the expression "It's none of your business" which our parents so despised and wanted in vain for us to stop using, they have all disappeared. Even the helpful chores which we did not do until we were asked, we are now trying to do before being asked, anticipating when our help is needed.

But now, what is this? "You don't have to know things like that." "If we report honestly, we will be unable to put food on the table."

In social studies we had decided, "Let's make the most accurate statistical chart we can do by ourselves," and we visited every household in different subsection blocks of the village. The result, contrary to what we had planned, was that we only found out which subsection contained the greatest liars. The teacher merely said, "It's okay. You did your best. The point is to think about it." And he was even smiling.

Well? What am I to think? What on earth should I be doing? The teacher says, "There absolutely should not be any deceit." Dad says, "Without trickery and the black market we cannot survive in today's world." Now, which is wrong?[1]

Yamabiko Gakkoo was a bestseller, made into a popular movie in 1952, and followed by many publications on the significance of the book. At a time when people in Japan were searching for resources to regain their own values and dignity, the powerful, down-to-earth writing of these students was like rain on a parched land. The general public was also impressed with the potential value of writing in all aspects of education. A term was coined for "seikatsu tsuzurikata–type education" in which personal writing was perceived not as a language arts discipline per se, but as a primary vehicle in all learning.

Meanwhile an organization of some 300 seikatsu teachers, *Nihon Tsuzurikata no Kai* (the Japan Tsuzurikata Association), was established in 1950 with its monthly journal *Sakubun Kenkyuu* (Composition Study). (The Association's name was changed to the present *Nihon Sakubun no Kai*—Japan Composition Association—in 1951, and the name of the journal to the present *Sakubun to Kyooiku*—Composition and Education—in 1952.) At the First National Composition Education Conference held at Nakatsugawa City in the Ena region in 1952, with 1,300 people attending, its organizational structure was reformulated to the present one, to be the national organization of the seikatsu movement. The membership of *Nihon Sakubun no Kai*, as of 1984, numbers approximately 10,000, and the circulation of its monthly journal about 14,000. The three-day national conference has, since 1952, been held every summer, at various conference sites. The number of those attending has ranged from thirteen hundred to thirty-five hundred people. The basic organizational structure for the preservation and enhancement of the seikatsu movement in Japan was thus set at the beginning of the 1950s.

According to Kazuo Isoda (1980:221), the postwar "golden age" of the seikatsu movement dated from 1951 to about 1958. But as the nationwide popularity of seikatsu tsuzurikata soared, cautions were also sounded. As early as 1951, the June 9 edition of *Asahi Simbun* (*Asahi News*) carried the following comment (as quoted in Ouchi 1984:180):

Language has both self-expressive and communicative functions. Therefore, it would not do to have children engage only in self-expression, i.e., seikatsu writing. The techniques to transmit information correctly, as in the cases of class news articles, study reports, memoranda, review essays, et cetera, must be properly taught also. This comprehensive extent must mark the new writing education. But, of course, the seikatsu training in grasping phenomena concretely and writing them concretely must constitute the basis upon which the other writing techniques can be built.

Friends and foes alike engaged in open debate with seikatsu proponents over the need for a systematically developed, functionally and technically oriented language-arts curriculum. The debate, perhaps the most publicized in the field of language-arts education in postwar Japan, continued heatedly for at least four years, 1952–55, without a clear resolution.

The fact was that most seikatsu teachers considered seikatsu tsuzurikata to be much more than a language-arts curriculum; for them, it had to do with real-life education that unified all subject matter in a critical way. However, times were changing. The most serious attack on the seikatsu movement in the postwar era came around the beginning of the 1960s from fellow teachers such as guidance specialists and teachers of science and mathematics. This was the Sputnik generation in Japan, as it was in the rest of the world. Seikatsu proponents were accused of overextending themselves by claiming expertise where they had no real systematic curricular plans to meet the latest demands in each of these disciplines. It was in response to these charges that a critical 1962 policy statement of *Nihon Sakubun no Kai* was issued. It called upon its members for a strengthening and systemizing of the language-arts aspects of seikatsu tsuzurikata and the avoidance of "arrogance" in assuming that other disciplines did not have their domain in education.

As for its own responsibility in the language-arts curriculum, the national association proposed in 1965 a five-step curricular outline, which will be discussed in chapters 14 and 15, as well as a particular sequence of lessons, which is described in chapter 12. All in all, this was a move toward accepting progress made in teaching methods in various disciplinary fields.

It was, however, a controversial move, and as time went by, it met with considerable criticism, both internal and external, of the seikatsu movement. It also caused some important regional seikatsu groups, as in Ena and Osaka, to break from the national association, at least temporarily. The Ena group, which had hosted the first national convention in 1952, went its own way, refusing the new policy's orientation toward "compartmentalization." And Ryuuji Nona of Osaka argued that standardization of writing education, even that proposed by the national association, could steer teachers' attention away from the need to deal with children's minds directly. As he put it (Nona 1983:127):

When we read children's writing, we should not be constrained by any preoccupation with skills or forms of their writing. What we must concentrate on above all else is the personhood of the child who has written it, his feeling, his lively mind trying to live to its limit. What we must see is whether the child's heart is burning within him. We must see clearly the particular reality that is his. That is where the fundamental importance lies in reading children's writing.

There are signs of reconciliation, however: since 1984, representatives from both Ena and Osaka have participated in national conventions. But some basic differences may still linger. At issue remains the underlying objective of the seikatsu movement: Is it language arts or is it self-actualization? At the level where seikatsu tsuzurikata has been most effective, the answer, it seems, has to be not either-or but a "yes" to both.

At the crux of the issue is still another basic question: What draws teachers into seikatsu tsuzurikata? Each seikatsu teacher would have a different story to tell. But the following autobiographical account by Masae Hanaoka may be a rather typical one (Hanaoka 1980:15–16, 20):

In 1949, April, I began my career as a teacher still looking very much like a young student myself. Kawabe Elementary School in a small village by the Chikuma River (in Nagano Prefecture) was the school I was assigned. I had chosen teaching without much conviction or confidence in myself as a teacher. But I became an elementary school teacher because I was drawn to children. It was a shaky beginning. . . . But the children called me "teacher," and seemed to like me. I was relieved. . . . I loved them. But I could not draw them out in my daily lessons. I had no skills, no means to do so. My own voice sounded to me too formal and self-gratuitous when I talked to them in class. My teaching was a rendition even in my own ears of ready-made patterns. I felt as though my voice slid right over the children's heads, struck the back wall, and came right back to hurt me. It was like this every day. . . . I wanted to quit teaching. . . . I learned to involve myself in mountain climbing, to get away from such concern. . . .

In 1954, I was at Kamishina Elementary School, which was my second assignment. We had a young teacher, Junshi Obikawa, . . . who, I later learned, was a proponent of seikatsu tsuzurikata. . . . He took over a class that I had taught for the previous three years, from first through third grade. He was making mimeographed copies of the children's journals and poems to hand them out for class use. And he left some on my desk. I looked at them. And I was shocked. There they were, the children, whom I had not been able to draw out, alive in those lines of their unadorned writing. Their natural voices were echoed in them. And in those drops of words, their real faces were reflected. I had had those children for three years in my class. I felt as though I was hit by a hammer, and I felt dizzy.

Seikatsu tsuzurikata remains a grass-roots movement in spite of its long history and powerful background because it is based on the needs of children and the desire of individual teachers to contribute to their welfare and education as fellow human beings, unhindered by whatever external demands might be imposed upon that relationship. Seikatsu tsuzurikata will survive and flourish as long as the movement continues to meet such a need.

TEACHER-STUDENT INTERACTION

CHAPTER **J** IF THAT IS A TOPIC,
I HAVE SOMETHING TO SAY TOO

CLEANING

We finished clearing the desks by pushing them to the front of the room. Nakayama-san was the first to get down on the floor. I put myself next to Nakayama-san, then Ikuta-san said "Me too" and got down beside me. Ishizawa-kun and Hirohara-kun were playing with their brooms. Katchin was by the lockers, legs stretched out.

Yesterday's classroom cleaning was our job. We did it with the Saito group.

Nakayama-san counted out, "1, 2, 3, 4, 5, 6, 7, 8, 9, 10" but I did only four strokes both ways. Because Nakayama-san's voice was coming to my ears so loudly I looked at her, wondering, "Is she really putting that much strength into it?" She had folded the cloth double, pushing it down firmly and looking hard at the cloth as she went "1, 2, 3, 4. . . ." There was sweat on the tip of her nose. Her face was red. I was working hard, but not as hard as she was.

While I looked at her admiringly, her actions suddenly slowed down and she raised her body and looked at her hands. She noticed that I was looking at her and she showed me her hands, saying, "Hmmm. I was putting so much force that my hands became really red." She had many little red spots on her hands.

Then after a little rest Nakayama began to rub again seeming to glare at the cloth.

Thinking I would do the same thing, I imitated her. Then sweat ran down behind my right ear.[1]

Etsuko's writing was presented in class as motivation for her fellow fourth graders. The assignment for which the students were being motivated was worded as follows: "Write about involvement with friends or teacher, going along with or going against, on a certain day at a certain time." This sort of broad theme is typical of the tasks set in seikatsu classes, where assignments are made in the course of a composition "unit." Etsuko had written about cleaning the classroom. She had captured a unique element from an everyday experience and had

broad theme

documented it minutely. That is just what is expected of the writer at an early stage of the typical seikatsu curriculum: a certain event of a certain time is selected, and the writer's detailing, especially sensory detailing, encapsulates the event into a text.

Kunio Kikuchi, Etsuko's teacher, says that other students will realize from this writing that they can do the same thing. In deciding upon a particular event, they need to look for something that happened once, even in the midst of routine occurrences. It may be as fleeting as Etsuko's momentary awareness, but something must distinguish it as having taken place at "a certain time." The students realize that Etsuko wrote not about the cleaning itself, but rather, "about the time I wanted to imitate Nakayama's way of cleaning" (Kikuchi 1977:105). Learning how to define the main idea may sound like a reading-class objective, but Kikuchi specifically distinguishes the reading of a composition such as Etsuko's from a reading lesson. The same reading ability may be utilized, he says, but the purpose "is not to comprehend the text, but to conduct the class so that the children get the feeling, 'Oh, I see, when I write I can write like this' " (p. 105).

Etsuko's conception of what constitutes a topic is probably a reflection of her training, but it also reveals what Graves calls "ownership." Graves talks about the difference in terms of revision, making an analogy between the kinds of repairs a homeowner will undertake as opposed to those a renter is usually willing to do. Etsuko's sense of control seems particularly evident in the precision with which she begins and ends her writing. Even before providing the context for the scene, she efficiently describes the posture of each member of the cleaning team. Then, with intense involvement, she documents a precise experience, beginning with the team leader's counting and ending exactly at the personally conclusive moment, the instant in which she also felt the sweat trickle down.

For an audience who would not understand the policy of school cleaning by students in Japan, Etsuko's writing might need expansion. On the other hand, with only her teacher and classmates as audience, Etsuko could confine her attention to such minutiae as the red spots on her teammate's hands or her own perception of the girl's expression as seeming to "glare at the cloth."

A topic for writing in the seikatsu curriculum exists in any mundane event that children encounter in their daily lives. And the choice of topic is the foundation of a connecting process that fosters the personal and cognitive development seikatsu teachers anticipate for their students.

In the writer-bias orientation, the reader's attention is not at stake, so the topic may be as mundane as picking an interesting flower or washing dishes. The writer's own interest is the standard by which to judge the merits of a possible topic. "Choose something that remains strong in your mind/heart" is the way children are told to make the decision. It is in realizing that one's life is so full of legitimate topics that the child begins to make writer-self–experiencer-self connections.

Teruo Tamiya, a seikatsu writing teacher and leader, relates how he took his second graders out for a nature walk and asked them to look for changes that had taken place since they were there the week

A. *Cleaning teams rotate responsibility for classroom, hall, principal's office, teachers' room, bathrooms, garden, and animals.*

B. *Cleaning is done daily.*

before. Then he walked among them, unobtrusively jotting down their comments. Later, back in the classroom, he reminded them of what they had said. For example,

Shinobu-chan, you were looking at the small violet seeds and you said, "Oh, they're so small. Eyes, little black eyes." You were surprised, weren't you? They were so small and shiny, just like small eyes. You may have forgotten that you said that, but, if written down like this, your words are always here (Tamiya 1968:9).

In this way he indicates the importance of retaining even the very small things that "moved one's heart" and opening one's mind to such things. This attitude underlies seikatsu writing.

Having identified the moment of insight, or memory, children extend their search to observe through recollection just what sensory and emotional details accompanied their experience. Writing regularly, especially in journals, conditions children to seek potential topics in daily events. The journal is not a documentary log of the entire day. Nor is it a rambling free-writing exercise. A journal entry should revolve around a meaningful event or moment of insight. But instead of directing it in those words, the teacher instructs students to choose as a topic something that "remains strong in your mind/heart" and to explore that topic fully through sensory memory and explicit description.

Writer-biased expectations enable children to evaluate events according to their own interest, without concern for captivating an audience. "Tell it just as it happened" and "Write it as it really was, remembering clearly how it looked and sounded at that time" are instructions that free the writer from obligations to engage in window dressing. A child who tries to include more than a single strong memory is encouraged to separate the writing into two pieces of writing and then to concentrate on only one at a time. The object is to strengthen the writer's connection to the event; in the process of writing, linkages that had been superficial are forged more solidly. That is a parallel between seikatsu education and the process approach advocated by Graves and others: children themselves pinpoint the aspect of their surroundings they will deal with. In journals especially, writers are freed from the risk of reader rejection, so they can turn freely to discover topics for which they can make their own connections through writing.

In addition to journal writing, children work in class on longer compositions. Often they refer to their journals to make topic choices, and they sometimes expand a journal entry into a full composition. We often saw children consulting their journals in the process of writing longer compositions.

Composition units often range over a week or two weeks, during which students study other children's compositions and write one of their own. (This sequence is described in chapter 12, "Lesson Planning.") Such a unit typically begins with a "motivation session," a lesson utilizing a child's composition (such as Etsuko's), which is expected to "raise the desire to write." The fact that the compositions used as models are clearly child-written increases self-confidence. Besides compositions available from that class or school, seikatsu teachers share compositions through association meetings and publication of class anthologies. But the composition used is always by a real child of approximately the same age as the students. This fosters the spirit of "If that's what writing is, I can do it too."

The teacher's effectiveness in facilitating topic choice is highlighted in motivation sessions. Of course all previous class discussion sessions and the teacher's comments have cumulative motivational powers. Yet there is presumed to be special inspiration in the way a teacher leads a class discussion of a child's composition. And, just as the teacher uses personal response to celebrate and illustrate to the individual child her accomplishment, so the teacher tries to lead the class to do the same by discussing the model composition.

The use of a model composition may have a slightly different objective in writer-biased education than in reader-biased composition training. Presumably, in a reader-biased orientation, either the contents or the technique so strike individual readers that they get an urge to produce a text for other readers. They imagine the "imprint" on those readers more readily for having just been imprinted by a text themselves. But, according to Etsuko's teacher, in a writer-biased context, readers look through the text to see the writer at work and say to themselves, "Oh, if that is what a writer does, I can do it too," or "If that is a topic, I have something to say too" (Kikuchi 1977:105).

It is that difference that separates writer bias from reader bias, and it manifests itself in a shifting of attention toward the activity of writing. This is why we see such parallels between the so-called "process approach" and the seikatsu writing curriculum. In the process approach children are frequently asked about their strategies for writing or making topic choices—attention is focused on their processes, instead of merely on their products. Many seikatsu teachers ask the students to use the text to make conjectures about the author's motivations, intentions, and strategies. Often, it is only after listening to the way their text conveyed these qualities to the audience that authors are given a chance to describe the history of the writing themselves.

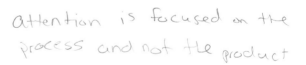
attention is focused on the process and not the product

CHAPTER **3** JOURNAL WRITING

It was only about a week after the beginning of school, but the first grader who created the drawing in Figure 1 was already able to explain in the writing under the picture:

April 14, Tuesday
I had a fight with my older sister and my sister took a brush and I said, What are you going to do? Then my sister threw the brush at me. It hit my arm and blood came out and I started to cry. At that time I hated her. The end.[1]

Along the side of the picture are the words, "Oh no she got me I thought."

His teacher, Kamemura, penned in a message to the writer and another to his mother (at the bottom left):

Toshihito, if the brush came flying, it must have hurt. It looks like a kind that would really hurt, doesn't it?

Mother, it's terrible to write about a fight with one's sister!! No, not at all. Look at it. Toshihito's feelings jump out of the page, don't they? For the seed idea of a journal what is best is what remains in the child's heart. What is important is what the child has chosen. "Oh no she got me I thought." It's wonderful writing, don't you think?

Toshihito's writing seems unusually explicit for a beginning first grader. Even without the drawing, this child described the event sufficiently for the teacher's understanding. But what gives life to the entry is the caption and the picture, in spite of the fact that they are unintelligible without the story. From the product we can imagine the look of satisfaction on Toshihito's face as he recreated the bristly weapon and added the words, "Oh no she got me I thought."

The seikatsu journal, both as a writing activity and as a discussion starter, is a primary tool for language arts as well as personal and cognitive development. As a writing activity it serves the child, deepening and enriching observational abilities and self-awareness. After it has served the child as a writing activity, it serves the teacher-child communication process. Then, when each child is given copies to study, some entries are used as resources for lessons.

Teachers often share interesting entries in a morning class meeting that opens the day. A more intensive sharing occurs when the teacher makes enough copies of an interesting entry for each student and uses it as the basis for an entire lesson. Whatever inspired one child enough to express becomes an opportunity for enriching the experience even more in a class discussion. This is not just for the writer's benefit but for the classmates as well. When bits of insight are multiplied by the thirty-five or more students who are given the task of reading and discussing the writer's perspective, everyone's observation and thinking is broadened and deepened. Kamemura describes the shift that occurs when a journal entry is reproduced for the others in the class: "One child's diary matter becomes every child's subject" (Kamemura 1971:138).

Figure 1

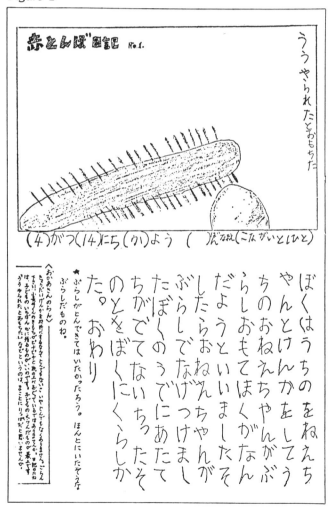

Kamemura encourages students to utilize each other's journals as seeds for their own writing. Although topics may always be freely chosen, children are allowed and encouraged to attempt some "imitation journals." Once when we were visiting his class, Kamemura distributed copies of a first grader's composition, at the end of which he had written, "Kaori noticed something special about the way people work near her house. Perhaps you can try to be more observant about work as well."

On another day's visit to his first-grade class, we watched as the first graders examined two other entries, which were reproduced under the heading "Imitation Journal." Kamemura had selected one by a boy who had written on January 21 about being unable to find snow boots his size. The boy reported his observation that the store, which was usually well stocked, had a surprisingly meager selection, probably because of the unusually snowy winter Tokyo was having. On February 3 a girl had written about how the neighborhood shopkeepers were setting out large displays of vegetables in the morning, but she had noticed that most of the vegetables were gone by the end of the day. This child had concluded that people shop closer to home instead of going to the supermarkets on snowy days. At the end of the paper on which these journal entries were copied were two discussion questions: "What sort of things did they notice?" and "After noticing these things, what did they think about them?" Finally, there was the "inspiration" for imitation: "Following these two models, what can you write as well?"

Picture Journal

Seikatsu writing education is neither content-driven nor skill-dominated. It is never too early to expect real-self expression, but there are skills that must await maturation and experience. The writer orientation takes precedence over skill development. Children who have not mastered the Japanese phonetic alphabet well enough, or have not clearly established their sounding-out abilities, are usually told to leave a circle for word parts they cannot determine.[2] The context provides teachers with enough clues to supply the missing phonetic characters themselves. It is at these early stages that a picture journal is considered especially useful, both for the child in self-expression and for the teacher in deciphering that expression. The teacher's job is to "read" both the picture and the words to decipher the "mind/heart of the child that the child wants to express."

The following diary entry, from September 22, 1983, written by Kaori Nakamura (shown in its original form in Figure 2), appeared in a collection that Kamemura made into a booklet of all the entries of that day:

This morning on the way to school on the train a stranger stepped on my foot. I did the same thing back to her and then she glared right at my face. I was embarrassed. She had glasses on. I was scared.

Figure 2

Kamemura wrote in the margin:

I guess the person who stepped on your foot did not say, "I'm sorry," did she, Kaori? I wonder what I would have done. I'd probably have ended up just taking it.

The picture shows a girl looking sheepish, but angry, and a woman with glasses looking at her hard. Hand straps, a seated figure, and the ceiling fan identify the train setting.

When Kamemura read Kaori's journal, he became a co-spectator of the train experience. Furthermore, he became a co-spectator of Kaori's moment of drawing because she left traces of a large figure, incompletely erased, stepping on the girl's toe. By looking closely he could tell that she changed her picture from a representation of the initial contact to a drawing of the finale. Kaori is a beginning writer, but she was not just practicing letter formation, sentence structure, or drawing. She had tried to express the confusion of a social conflict. Her teacher "read" into her drawing and writing (including the redrawing of the scene) Kaori's sense of uncertainty. Kamemura acknowledged both the injustice and the fact that there were at least two ways to have reacted, Kaori's retaliation or silent suffering. He did not make any judgment, but he put himself in the position of sharing her indecision about the best course in that situation.

On the same day that Kaori wrote in her journal about the train incident, her classmate, Hitoshi, wrote about seeing a "television taxi."

His picture had little elaboration. Kamemura ignored the lack of detail both in the writing and in the picture, but praised the pride in investigative accomplishment that he sensed as being the mind/heart that this boy wanted to express. Hitoshi wrote:

> *Yesterday when I was standing at my bus stop a television taxi really went by and I looked to see if there really was a television and there really was. It was really wonderful. I was happy because it was the first one I saw. I was very happy and it was really good. It was so wonderful.*

Kamemura responded:

> *It is good that you can look at something so well. Wanting to understand how it really was, you were truly happy when you could find out for yourself. When we discover things, it makes us very happy, doesn't it?*

As the child attains greater fluency, the pictures begin to recede in importance. They become less graphic as the child acquires descriptive ability. By comparing picture content and text content, the teacher can tell when the child is ready to discontinue pictures. According to Kamemura, this usually happens sometime in the latter part of first grade.

Journals Grow Up with the Child

Once established into a routine, journals are usually written as homework and submitted to the teacher on a regular basis. Some teachers, especially in the first two grades, collect and read them daily, but many teachers of older students lighten the load for themselves by collecting journals from a predetermined group on Monday, a different group on Tuesday, etc.

A perennial problem for teachers who want their students to keep a journal and who want that activity to have personal and cognitive benefits for the children is whether to make the task compulsory.

Teachers are always eager to hear how others solve the problem of the reluctant diarist. Kamemura describes how he straddles the line between compulsion and freedom by requiring not that children write, but that they submit their journals to him on schedule (Kamemura 1979:117–23). Their obligation is to turn in the journal on time, whether a new entry has been added or not. In this way, no special attention is given to the student who has not actually written.

When journals are returned, every child turns eagerly to find what the teacher has to say, and the child who did not write finds that, on the page that was left blank, Kamemura has written a message anyway. It is not a complaint and does not appeal to any sense of guilt. These responses are hard to write, Kamemura admits, but he says that it can be made easier by realizing that you speak to that child every day, so you are just doing some of that speaking in writing instead. You cannot answer what has not been written, but there are aspects of the child's life experience that you would want to respond to as if the child had written them.

Kamemura points out that it is the content of the child's life to which he responds the most, so the teacher's challenge is to search out some experience of commonality to write about as a response to the child. For example, the following writing by Kamemura filled an otherwise blank page in the journal of a child who had neglected to write:

Tatsuo, today's home run you made [in kickball] was terrific! Clearly, just as I said, by not kicking from the side, right away it was an improvement. When you do that, it really flies. Doing it really made it go far. A little more and it would have gone into the gym. I think, however, I could make it go still farther. (Kamemura, p. 120)

Sometimes, he says, you have to search your memory to think of incidents from several days before and, if nothing occurs to you, write one-sidedly, initiating a topic you would like to bring up. For example:

Recently it has become warm, hasn't it? Jiro, for you kids nowadays it might not be the same as it was for me, but when I was a kid, as soon as the weather got warm like this, we would wade in the stream and try to catch fish and freshwater clams. The water was clean and only came up to our ankles in the shallow parts. When I got lots of clams, my mother made soup from them. The clams were small and had a beautiful light brown color. (Kamemura, p. 121)

He reports that few children can resist writing at least a line or two after reading about three of these messages. However small, their few lines become the seed for another response. He warns that there are some children who are so "thick-skinned" as to resist writing while enjoying his comments anyway. If that is the case, he suggests that teachers should still consider their response as an opportunity for life guidance and do it ungrudgingly. As proof of its value, he points to the obvious pleasure with which even nonwriters delve into their journals, looking for his comments. Tamiya reminds his colleagues: "This work is not unlike making stone walls by piling one rock on another, but the more steady, detailed, and continuous that piling is, the more certain is the strength, and the less likely to tumble down" (Tamiya 1983:24).

The teacher may sympathize with the fact that filling blank pages can be an onerous task and, as Kamemura does, give hints to help those who need some gentle jostling to shake loose an idea. Some hints challenge students to develop new writing skills. A part of Kamemura's blackboard is reserved for these hints, and a new one appears every few days, sometimes illustrated by a sample, which he shares from his stock of writing by former students. Here are some he gave a class of second graders near the beginning of the school term: "May 17. When you write the speech of the teacher or your friends, are you putting quotation marks? If you do, the meaning will be clearer and it will be easier to read." "May 19. Some of you have been buying those green bugs, watching them every day and writing about them in your journals. Have the appearance and colors begun to change?" "May 25. Today in school, what were the times you volunteered to speak? At those times how did other students react to what you said?" (Kamemura 1971:176).

As students reach the upper elementary grades their journal entries reflect the changes that are occurring developmentally. Their social awareness is brought to bear on the journal in a variety of ways. Using journal entries and compositions as models maintains the pace of natural modification.

In upper elementary grades some children begin to explore their own thinking about controversial issues and problems in society, basing some entries on information and impressions gained from reading books, watching television, and the like. Their early training of writing their own reactions assures that their voice will be present even when the subject matter moves from primary to secondary involvement with the topic. At the same time that such maturing begins to show itself in the writing of students in upper intermediate and junior high school grades, teachers also notice an increasing self-consciousness. Students begin to self-edit material that might have been submitted freely at a younger age. Whether or not they maintain a personal journal for their own purposes, they no longer tend to blurt out life experiences in the school-assigned journal.

When this transformation occurs, teachers may change the format to accommodate the difference. In addition, they may transfer some of the responding activity to classmates, adding opportunities for students to react while maintaining their own part in response as well.

Terumoto Asahina described how a group journal serves his fifth graders (1976:33–34). He divides students into groups of four. On the first day, student A writes and the teacher, after inserting his comments, gives the journal to student B. Student B writes an entry to which the teacher responds and gives the diary to student C, and so on. When all four have had a turn, the journal goes back to student A, who, using a page divided into three parts, responds to students B, C, and D. Then B has a turn at responding to A, C, and D, and so forth. After that, the cycle begins again. Asahina says that, at the beginning of the term, students comment most on mechanics and the appearance of the pieces, such as the darkness of the pencil or the placement of quotations on the lines, but then, as the term goes on, they begin to react more and more to the content and give their own impressions.

In junior high school, some variation of the "revolving journal" is particularly time-saving for a teacher who may have three or more language-arts classes a day. On a given day only a portion of the students have their turn at writing in the journals that make the rounds in each class.

65

Journal Writing

Isamu Ariki shared the following samples of a revolving journal in a circle-group meeting. We were amused to notice the (perhaps universal) adolescent sense of drama in these ninth-graders' entries.

COMPOSITION AND ME

"All right. Your turn." Mr. Ariki handed me the revolving journal. I mentally freaked out. "Ugh, it's my turn."

Going back in time a little, it was the first language arts class. Mr. Ariki said, "From now on I would like you to write in something like this," and he raised a journal notebook high and gave it to the first student. At that time that journal notebook struck me like a troublesome cliff looming in front of me and blocked me from seeing anything else.

Why? That's because I have "super-despised" (I mean to indicate that I have hated more than hate . . .) compositions since elementary school days. When I have composition paper in front of me, inside my head becomes like a hodge-podge and somehow I end up getting depressed. And it takes ten minutes to decide on the title. When it is bad I think for 10 to 15 minutes never finding any good title and ending up not handing anything in. (For your information, I have not touched this journal notebook for two days since I got it. And it took ten minutes to think of the title.)

But having a title is no big consolation. When the title gets decided, the first five or six lines and the last words come floating to me. So I write a little, but it doesn't continue on so I fall into deep thinking. Then somehow I survive and complete it. But, by the time it is over, it's about 30 minutes since the beginning, if things go well, and nearly one hour when things do not go so well. This composition has taken 30 minutes. "I hate compositions. Really hate them." Written April 19, 1984.

On the same day, in a revolving journal in Ariki's second-hour class, another ninth grader wrote the following:

MY ROOM

Now, happening to look around my room, I realize that the scene has been changing at a dizzying pace. It has changed a great deal even since my entrance into junior high.

There are various things which were not here when I entered junior high. CB radio, little bedside table, for example. There are other things that weren't here then. The school uniform which I took off when I came home, the clothes I took off when I got wet walking the dog, textbooks and other things, all scattered around. These weren't here when I entered junior high.

When I think of it, it seems that "my room" reflects the change of "my personality." The scattering of books and clothes that I mentioned may have happened because a tendency for "can't be bothered" has grown in "my personality." This "can't be bothered" which has grown in my personality may have contributed to my

*drop in grades. I hope to return "my room" and "my personality"
to the time I started junior high and with the feeling of a new start
do better in the coming year. Written April 19, 1984.*

Aside from the fact that the revolving journal seems to work better in upper grades because of student attitudes and busy schedules, the revolving or shared-task journal also marks an adjustment in the writer-reader issue. From the beginning there existed a trusted audience, but the journal was a separate volume for each child. In the group journal, one volume represents the group. No matter how personal the writing, it is contained within the same cover as writing done by others. Sometimes one piece of writing is a response to another. Especially for pre-adolescents this is a significant extension of self as writer toward reader-biased writing, even though the genre continues to be largely personal narration.

In summary, then, journals and journal-like writing, albeit to an audience, form the basis of seikatsu writing. Even though people have a natural tendency to shield their thoughts and feelings from others as they grow older, the journal continues to provide an outlet, changing its nature with the developing student.

CHAPTER 4 THE AKAPEN

We have a term in English "to red-pen" something, meaning to analyze and illuminate its features, often the negative ones, objectively and critically. The Japanese translation of "red pen" is *akapen* (AH-KAH-PEN), but to *akapen* someone's writing has a diametrically opposite meaning in seikatsu circles: to highlight features, especially positive ones, subjectively and spontaneously. When seikatsu teachers "red pen" a student's work, they are not evaluating or criticizing; rather, they are playing the part of a sensitive and caring reader. The teacher's responses in the margins and at the ends of students' writing represent the other side of the writing act, the reception of the words and image formation in a reader's mind. The purpose of the responses, therefore, is not strictly praise, but corresponds most closely to what a co-spectator might think upon becoming privy to the event being described. It also corresponds to the way an encouraging friend might nurture a speaker's self-expression by "back-channeling" (for example, by murmuring assent or nodding). One of the effects of back-channeling is to maintain contact while acknowledging that the speaker continues to have the floor—in other words, to honor the fact that the speaker is speaking. Similarly, the akapen's primary function, as curriculum specialist Kazuo Takeda told us, is to honor the fact that the child is writing. This is a far cry from the bloodletting function that has come to be so associated with red-penning in English that some teachers actually avoid red ink entirely.

As in the following writing by a second grader in Hiroko Iwatani's class, the akapen commentary sometimes back-channels and sometimes interacts, just like a listener in a rather one-sided dialogue. Applying these speech acts to written expression has the psychological effect of putting reader and writer into the same time frame, the time of the writing act.

July 6, Tuesday.
　About my name Makoto, my mother and father say "Ma means 'really' and Koto is because we want you to be gentle-hearted."

(akapen)
Makoto, your parents thought this when they named you, didn't they? It sure is a good name. The koto is an old Japanese instrument with a gentle sound.

I like my name but I hate being teased about it.

The first time we were going home together when Mitani-kun said, "This. She's Makoto" and some people I didn't even know said "Makoto. Only boys are Makoto" and "Really, there are no girls with that name." At that time I cried.

Recently Suda-kun and a person about third grade came following me, saying in a soft voice, "A girl, huh. Makoto, huh. Strange, isn't it?" They stopped when they got right behind me. Then I wanted to cry but I held it back and ran on home. Then, "I'm home" I said in a tearful voice and when I saw my mother's face I started crying right away.

At that my mother told me, "Makoto, when I was little I was teased too, '1000 needles, 1000 needles' and I hated it, but now it is a good memory." And I stopped crying.

Well, even so, my mother might remember it as a good memory, but I Makoto do not like it, I thought. Therefore, although I really like my name, because I really hate being teased about it, from now on please don't do it.[1]

You like the name but you were teased.

You are writing remembering well the words you heard, aren't you?

Resentful tears. What about Mitani and the others then, I wonder.

Were you teased again?! If you get teased so much you would get resentful.

You came back holding in the tears, but when you looked at your mother, you couldn't hold back any more, right?

I see that your mother had also been teased. She comforted you saying that it would become a good memory. I'd want you to explain why she was called 1000 needles.

The last line seems like Makoto's request to everyone.

The intimate relationship between writer and akapen wielder is maintained by the sensitivity of the akapen response. Like a good listener the akapen writer must be attentive to nuances. Unlike face-to-face communication, however, the akapen response has limited nonverbal options. The most common nonverbal written response might be the underlining of particularly effective parts, which some teachers use along with a written comment in the margin. But that cannot compare to the multitude of nonverbal responses available in conversation. We may speculate that what might seem to be mere echoing of the writing by the akapen response (as in the example above, "You like the name but you were teased") is actually the equivalent of a nod or raised eyebrow in a face-to-face conversation.

Seikatsu writing teachers consider the role of the akapen vital. Books and articles are written by teachers who have a reputation for skill in writing akapen commentary. Class anthologies, which are also distributed to colleagues, include the accompanying akapen comments. The national organization of seikatsu writing teachers annually honors anthologies that contain skillful akapen writing. Teachers study each other's akapen styles. Just like the skill of a good midwife, there is a knack to akapen writing that can be acquired but is difficult to explain. After tips are shared, the rest comes from practical experience.

One recommendation is to refer to the child by name as in conversation. Furthermore, as many teachers pointed out to us, the image of the child's face should be kept in mind by the person writing the akapen response so that the message will unconsciously take on a personal note. Before opening the journal, it pays to take a few seconds to call to mind the most immediate memories of that child, rather than to plunge into the reading and then check later to see whose name is on the cover. In keeping with this practice, they said, a set of rubber stamps, no matter how cute or complete, can never fulfill the akapen's role.

The akapen response should not be empty praise. It should be specific enough for the child to know exactly why the teacher reacted that way. Even though teachers describe the function as "praising" and "encouraging," the effect is more like that of a slightly flattering mirror. From the elaboration in the akapen commentary, children get a better look at what they accomplished. For example, even in a positive response, the writer is told specifically what strength has been revealed: rather than writing "Wonderful" in the margin, the akapen response is, "It is wonderful how carefully you remembered your father's exact words."

The tone must not be one of evaluation, even though praise may be freely included. Evaluatory interjections such as "Wow," "Terrific," and "Good" along the side of the page have the effect of stamping "Product" on the text. Strangely, using single-word interjections to respond to writing seems to indicate that the writing is over and the reader has taken charge; in contrast, a comment such as "You really used your eyes and ears to see and hear just how it was" seems to convey the impression that the writer still has control, because the remark relates directly to the process and only indirectly to the product.

The akapen writer doesn't focus only on positive attributes. Deficiencies, however, are usually described by referring to their effect upon a friendly reader. And, though gentle, the akapen response makes clear just what that reader lacks. Rather than simply inserting a question mark near some confusing section, the akapen responder is likely to muse, "What about Mitani and the others then, I wonder." Problems can even be dramatized: "When . . . because . . . when . . . because . . . ! Ono-kun, your diary is interesting, but I began to pant when I tried to read it" (Kamemura 1971:150–51).

The tone of the akapen responder is that of an over-the-shoulder kibbitzer: "You are really pursuing directly what you don't understand,

aren't you?'' or "This is the part you most wanted to write, I think.''
Sometimes the stance seems to be that of a friend reading an early
draft, even though the child may not actually deal with that topic again:
"I'd want to know why she was called '1000 needles.' " Most of all,
the response should sound like that of an intimate audience, as closely
involved in the writing process as a separate reader can be.

Children may begin to internalize this kibbitzer so that they anticipate
the response during the actual drafting of a piece. This is a form of
what Graves calls "forward vision," the anticipation of the imprint of
the words upon an audience. Ultimately, it is upon this imprint that
writers thrive.

We are calling this kind of writing "writer-biased prose" because the
teacher so controls the readership that the writer is protected from
generalized audience demands. Yet there might be debate about when
the audience factor becomes dominant enough to turn writer-biased
prose to reader-biased writing. Certainly children's conception of an
audience develops as they read the akapen notes and hear their own
and their classmates' writing as it is shared in class. Without these
regular and rather systematized audience experiences, young writers
might not learn to balance audience demands with a continuing sense
of self. The seikatsu writing teacher tries to maintain control over the
shift of focus that includes a readership, but does not deny that it will
occur.

The risk-taking that accompanies the growing consciousness of audience is fostered by the supportive akapen. It is an enabling experience
for writers to get a line-by-line corroboration of their written expression.
Furthermore, the akapen feedback is tangible. Spoken words certainly
are more direct, but they usually must be retained in memory. Children
who face the loneliness of a new writing task can reread the evidence
of past success as many times as they like. They can even share it
with parents at home, which incidentally tends to teach parents how
to become nurturers of the writing process as well. In the West we
are prone to choose oral routes of communication whenever there is
a choice. Yet even 30 students can tax our available conferencing
time. The akapen is a flexible alternative for some of the teacher-
student interaction in the classrooms. It enables us to join each child
in the writing act in a way more true to the reader-writer relationship
than conferencing, which actually represents a type of editor-writer
relationship.

The spectator stance usually expected of a seikatsu reader is one
that Britton contrasts with a stance called "participant," that is, a reader
expected to be involved as a result of the writing (see, for example,
Britton 1977 for further explanation of these terms). In the composition
by Makoto, there is an uncommon example of persuasive writing in
a beginning writer's seikatsu text: "Therefore, although I really like my
name, because I really hate being teased about it, from now on please
don't do it." The rest of her composition seemed to be written in a
spectator mode, that is, Makoto was reliving her experiences and simply
letting the reader in on her connection with reality. The akapen response,
as the teacher's moment-by-moment reaction, reflected a co-spectator

relationship until that last sentence. Then the response, like the composition, shifted to the class as an audience to be influenced: "The last line seems like Makoto's request to everyone." If, as is likely, this second grader shifted her stance on a last-minute impulse to appeal to her audience, the akapen response also reflects, perhaps, a last-minute decision by the teacher to share this writing with the other students. The shift in audience expectations in both cases was from the spectator stance (describing what happened) to the participant stance (making demands on the reader). Even if the ending was pre-planned, the strategy was to draw upon the readers' emotions through expressive writing that pulls at the heartstrings and then to elicit co-operation in a sudden switch to persuasive writing in the closing plea.

Most of the time the akapen commentary reflects the spectator stance. The responder can do this by taking one of two perspectives. One is to act as a co-spectator with the writer, reliving as an onlooker what the writer has experienced: "What a wonderful older sister!" or "Resentful tears." The other is to use the present progressive to comment on the writing experience. It is like holding a mirror up to the child in the course of the writing activity, even though the writing time has passed: "You are beginning by explaining when this happened" or "You are making clear just how frightened you were at the time." There is something timeless about a text that allows us to talk about it as an ongoing process. We do somewhat the same thing in talking about literature when we say, "Here Shakespeare is allowing his character to speak directly to the audience." Perhaps the akapen commentator is more audacious with the student than we dare to be with Shakespeare, for the akapen response has omniscient overtones for pedantic purposes. "You are thinking about the many ways that things change when winter comes." Perhaps, just as children present themselves in the light in which they would like to be seen, akapen responses reflect the image in which teachers would like children to see themselves. In so doing, they hope that in the future children will deliberately live up to what may have been a subconscious or coincidental success. That is the reinforcing effect of the akapen.

CHAPTER **10** FOUR EVALUATORY STANDARDS

The basic local units in the seikatsu organization are the circle groups that meet to provide support for members of a given geographical area. These groups meet at least monthly and function as an arena where educational theories can be developed in the course of discussing specific compositions. Those we attended in and around Tokyo proved to be some of our richest resources.

The teachers described in chapter 4, who grappled with the evaluation of Masami's composition "The Day Grandpa Cried" were *Tokyo Sakubun Kyooiku Kyoogikai* (the Tokyo Writing Education Conference), a group made up of each leader of the smaller circle groups all over Tokyo. On the same day that they discussed Masami's writing, they also discussed a sixth-grade girl's composition, in which she details her three attempts at school election success, the first two of which were resounding failures. The following excerpt describes Kazuko's third venture into school politics:

THE THIRD TRY

. . . In the middle of the third term came the election for student council members. "Kazuko-chan, are you going to do it this time?" "No, I am not going to. Because, if I fail, the boys are going to tease me." "But this time you are going to be elected for sure."

Thinking back, when I had been crying at home because I was so hurt by the boys' teasing, my parents had said to me, "If you have to cry that much, don't run for office any more." I decided then, "I will never run for office again." But, inside, I did want to be an officer. However, if I'd run again and fail, I was not going to like the boys' teasing. I wrote about it in my journal. Then the teacher said to me, "Why don't you run once more for student council?" I was encouraged by these words from the teacher, and from what my friends said. I then decided to run. I went home and said, "My friends are encouraging me. I am going to run again." Grandma said that it would be fine for me to run but I was not to be too discouraged if I failed. I said, "I will be okay." . . .

I was determined, "This time I am going to be elected." And I put in five or six times more effort on my campaign than I had be-

*fore. Okamoto-san, who became my sponsor, cooperated with me
and worked hard too.*

*"I am running for the vice presidency. Can I get your support?" I
asked the 6th graders during basketball practice and anyone I knew.
There were four candidates for the office of vice president. The
number one enemy among them was Teruyo Kato. Her votes in
the last election were a lot higher than mine. I remembered that
and was anxious, thinking that I might fail. But I chased the anxiety
away with a feeling of determination that I would never surrender.*

*On election day I was feeling light-hearted from morning on. Dur-
ing my time off, I went around through the 4th graders' classes with
Takemoto-san and others. And finally came the time for formal
speeches. My turn is the third among the candidates for female vice
president. "I wish my turn would come quickly." But, as my turn
comes closer, my heart begins to pound stronger, thump, thump.
One gets nervous even for the third time. I told myself that I'd better get calmed down.*

*"For the same office, Kazuko Shibata." "Yes." I stood up and
went up to the middle of the platform. "How are you, everyone." I
said without thinking, "I have failed twice already, so you must be
thinking that it's about time I should stop running. But I am not
going to give up yet . . ." I said what I believed very clearly and
loudly. "Please support Kazuko Shibata."*

*When the speech was over, I felt relieved. But the thump, thump
of my heart was still going on. The formal speeches were over before we knew it. The election committee members were collecting
votes. Kato-san and I said to each other, "It's now already been
decided, hasn't it?"*

*We went back to the classroom. While working on a woodblock
print, I thought that they must now be counting the votes, and I
worked on. Every time the classroom door opened, scree scree, my
eyes went over there, thinking that it may be an election committee
member. When a boy, who had been making sly comments before,
said to me "I voted for you, so be thankful," it really made me
happy.*

*I wondered what I'd do if I did not make it. But, mainly, I had a
feeling that I might possibly make it because lots of people supported me.*

*More than one hour has already passed since then. The door
opened, scree scree. Nakane-san entered and was reporting something to the teacher. Hearing it, I locked my hands together, "I
made it!" I jumped with joy with Okamoto-san and Hatsuka-san.
"We made it, we made it!" But I was still worried a little wondering
if I really became the vice president. My votes were 375. It was a
number I could hardly believe. My friends also said to me, "It's
great." "Congratulations." I smiled. Besides me, Ohta-kun and
Takemoto-san were elected. Aoo-kun was a runner-up.*

*I went home in a hurry. I said in a loud voice, "I made it!"
Mother did not believe me at first. But, when she found out that it
was true, she hugged me and jumped for joy. Grandma shook*

*hands with me saying, "You made it!" When Father came home
that night, I mentioned it to him with a smile. He did not believe
me at first, just like Mother. But, when Mother told him the news
again, he came running to me with a big smile, saying, "You really
succeeded?!"*

*Mother said to me, "You have to work hard, you know. Not just
in name only." That night, my heart was really filled with joy.*

*Next morning, when I was going to school, I felt as though a
burden was off my shoulders and my feet were lighter. I felt as
though I was in a different world. I felt really fine. I could really get
myself into it when our drill team practiced too. I am very happy
that I did not stop at the second failure.*

*"To fail is the beginning of success." That is really true. Soon,
the student council will begin. I am going to work hard.*[1]

The following transcription of the group discussion actually covers
only the major points, without their elaboration. It illustrates how the
teacher-leaders considered the composition both in the light of its
written effectiveness and in the shadow of a possible deficit in the girl's
understanding of political responsibility.

PRESENTER: I like this piece very much. Where necessary, the writer
has used a great deal of detail, but it is not overwritten.

TEACHER 1: There is clear proof of the writer's maturity in the way she
reports the three speeches she made. In her description of the
first speech, she remembers clearly; this goes with the extensive
detail about her disappointment at losing. The second speech is
reported in short but clear description, which goes with the lack-
adaisical attitude she took on her second attempt. Then, the third
speech is quoted directly. There is no overzealous description. As
a result the piece is extremely effective and gives the impression
that the writer is well trained in seikatsu tsuzurikata.

TEACHER 2: Well, I have to compare it to a composition written by a
third grader in Tamiya's class, in which the writer clearly specified
why she sought election. It lacks description of her intention. That
is regrettable.

PRESENTER: That is too much to ask of the writer. It is a matter of the
teacher's leadership. He should have done a better job of preteaching
about political responsibility. That is why students run for office.

TEACHER 2: But the question is the lack of vision at the time of deciding
to run for office. That should be there.

TEACHER 3: Perhaps that is a concern you have, but it was not something
the writer was concerned about.

TEACHER 4: The writer's motivation to run for office the first time, as
expressed in the beginning, is suspicious.

TEACHER 5: This writing isn't really about those things. It is about the
development of the writer, overcoming her inner conflict. Her
inner self developed as a result of the two failures and the final
success. That's why the title she chose was "The Third Try."

TEACHER 6: The greatest shortcoming is the fact that this composition is too individualistic. It is not appropriate to use as a discussion starter in class because the only ones described as really being happy over the outcome of the election were the family members. Even though she was elected, her relationship to her classmates is not made clear.

VISITOR: Isn't the issue really what is a valuable topic? What are valuable materials to use as one's subject?

TEACHER 7: From the viewpoint of personal development, it is appropriate material.

TEACHER 2: In my class we read this one and the one by the student in Tamiya's class, both with a positive response. I do believe that the vision involved in running for office is the teacher's responsibility, not just a matter of student initiative or desire.

TEACHER 7: Well, that is so, but actually it is hard to achieve.

As the first speakers indicated, the composition could be esteemed highly as an example of mature student writing. The problem cited by the teachers was not a writing problem as much as it was an ethical issue about her sense of responsibility. Without a clearly stated vision, should the girl's example be made a model for other students? Can the reader share the happiness of a girl if her ambition was perhaps too personal? The evaluation descended from praise for the writing to doubt about the writer's value system because the discussants included self-actualization objectives with writing-development goals.

We can postulate that there are four major categories that characterize the evaluatory statements made in the seikatsu circle-group meetings we attended. These categories represent our own interpretation of evaluatory types; they have not been so defined, as far as we can determine, in seikatsu literature or policy. The nature of the evaluatory statements we heard and read were so consistent, however, we assume that we are also postulating some of the actual objectives of the educational process. The attributes that teachers look for in compositions must also represent some of the goals of the writing education itself.

Without any ranking or order, these are the four general headings under which we could describe evaluatory standards: sincerity, authority, expression, and social responsibility. Sincerity relates to the motivation of the writer, and authority, to the writer's direct involvement with reality. Expression can be understood as success at either written or self-expression, and social responsibility goes beyond the writer and the writing to include the experience itself.

In the case of the girl who wrote about her election success on "The Third Try," there were teachers who judged her to have been successful by all standards except social (in this case, political) responsibility. They did not question her motivation to write, but rather her motive in seeking election. Even those who questioned her political motivation were willing to concede that this probably could be seen as an omission on the part of the teacher.

In looking at the composition "The Day Grandpa Cried" (chapter 4), all standards were considered met. Masami's sense of social responsibility was evidenced by her relationship with family members and by her response to the teachers' challenge that she be sure to get her grandfather there. Her sincerity and authority could be judged by inferring from the text her faithful intention to present reality and by her actual contact with that reality to begin with. In other words, it was her own reality she was describing and not someone else's, and she told the story without distortion or ulterior motive. In this instance, at least, she seemed to fit the ideal of a "whole person" who was grounded in reality and at one with society and mankind, and she was able to express selfhood in effective writing. By the yardsticks of sincerity, authority, expression, and social responsibility, Masami's connection-making through writing was a success.

The following composition raised the authority question briefly in the minds of some of the teachers at the Tokyo group leaders' meeting. Some wondered if perhaps the boy was inadvertently telling not his own story, but that of the leader of the boys, whose presence dominated the group. Others argued that the writer was directly involved in both the telling and the action, even though he seemed not to have fully resolved his relationship to the leader. Evidence of the boy's self-awareness was the detailed description, which was felt to be a result of both his training in writing and of his sense of selfhood.

MULBERRY GATHERING

This evening we went mulberry gathering beyond the bamboo groves near my house. It was me, Takuji, Kooji, Yasufumi and Michihiro. . . .

I wanted to hand the hat to Takuji so I called out, "Hey, Takuji." Then Takuji, with a face that seemed to say "Oh, finally!" dropped the mulberries in the hat. I held onto the hat with the mulberries in it and said, "Can I pick some too? because it is not fun just climbing the tree." Takuji was very involved in picking the berries and said, "Okay," absentmindedly. I began to pick berries near me. The berries were soft and looked easily crushable. I picked them carefully with my index finger and thumb and put them in Yasufumi's hat. There were no more berries around me so I said to Takuji, "Steer that branch there toward me," and Takuji said, "Where? Where?" "Toward the tip of the branch where you are standing." "Oh, this one?" Takuji said, but he was busy picking his own berries and did not give me the branch. So I stretched my hand as far as I could, after climbing a little higher, and I broke the branch with a big noise. Takuji said in a surprised voice, "Hey, it's dangerous! Don't go around making big noises near me."

I said, "Sorry," and I began to pick the berries from the broken branch. . . . I looked down and there was the river in front of my eyes. I thought, "If I fall, that will be the end of me," and I was frightened. I did not notice this when I was climbing up the tree, but when I was going down, I was aware of the river and I was a little scared. I held the hat with my mouth and went down, step by step, holding on to each branch. But, when I went down a little bit, there were no more branches. There was bamboo nearby so I used it and I got down to the ground, making my body like a ball.

The hat which I had held in my mouth almost dropped, so I bit down on the brim and regained my balance.

Takuji saw this and shouted, "Hey, Yasufumi, come here." By the time Yasufumi came to the foot of the tree, I had reached the ground and was at peace.

Takuji came down quickly and easily, as though making a lie out of the fact that I had so much trouble coming down.

We passed through the bamboo grove and a farm and went to a place where there was the remains of a campfire. Takuji said proudly, "Okay, everyone can eat." Everyone went "Yay!" and began to grab the berries and gobble them up. Takuji called out to Michihiro, who was in the rear, and said gently, as though noticing him suddenly, "Ah, Michihiro, you eat too." Because this added one other person, the mulberries disappeared quickly. At the bottom of the hat there was a black stain of mulberry juice. When Takuji said, "Oh, oh, the hat has gotten to be like this," everyone laughed. When I looked at Yasufumi he looked like he was either about to laugh or to cry. Takuji said, "Sorry, Yasufumi." Yasufumi said, "Um." He looked like it was okay then.

It was getting dark and there was the noise of the river.[2]

The classification of evaluatory standards that we are calling "authority" seems particularly important to seikatsu philosophy because children are expected to write from their own direct experience, something in which they were personally involved. This writer might have had an authority problem in his relationship to Takuji which caused the teachers to question the authority of his writing as well. However, they concluded that it was his own reality that he was describing, and not Takuji's. In order to bond oneself to reality, it is necessary to tell one's own story even in a situation like this, in which another character played a dominating role.

If the boy had used his experience as a basis for a creative-writing activity such as we often encourage in America, he might have improvised upon the outcome, basing a plot upon the incident but providing the reader with a sense of resolution by having the subject of the story either face up to, or put down, Takuji's dominance. Accommodating a reader's desire for a positive resolution is often a trait of children's stories. Furthermore, if the mulberry-picking story were reader-biased prose, it might need to have some of the details eliminated because they are superfluous to the plot. But in seikatsu writing, at least through elementary school, plot development is not the issue; the writer presents a personal view of reality with the authority that it is that writer's actual experience. Any thirst for justice on the part of the audience is not a consideration and, until there is a positive outcome in reality, the reader will have to accept what is still unresolved. One of the reasons that seikatsu compositions are described as being other than literature is that self-actualization objectives call for writing that does not curry the reader's favor by improving upon reality. For these reasons, sincerity and authority are fundamental requirements from which the writing is done. Similarly, truth telling, not fiction, is the norm for children's writing.

The following composition, discussed in another meeting by the same teacher-leaders' group, failed to satisfy the majority of evaluators in any of the four categories we have postulated as evaluatory standards. The teachers expressed consternation over flippancy in the writer's style, overdramatization (which could be seen as improvisation upon reality), and a lack of family (social) responsibility. The boy's fluency was seen negatively, as a ''running away of the pen, which must be crushed before he can grow.'' In terms of whether or not such superficial fluency is an obstacle to self-growth or writer growth, another teacher declared, ''This is not just a matter of expression style; training in expression style is training in a life-style that analyzes and focuses clearly.'' As for family responsibility, the teachers stated that they would have preferred that the boy had cleaned the tub in anticipation of his father's enjoyment of a clean bath rather than in fear of a scolding. One wonders if the writer's style would have irritated them so much had he described a more virtuous attitude, which could be held up for other children to emulate. Personal-development objectives complicate evaluation in a case such as this. But the teachers we talked to insist that the writing suffers when a child's sense of drama overwhelms his honest attempts to connect to reality. Therefore they discourage the dramatic flair in writing such as this:

CLEANING THE BATH

"Tooru, change the bath water," my mother said while washing rice, when I was doing my homework. I said, disagreeably, "Aw, today is Satoru's turn, so I don't want to." Mother said, in an angry voice, "Satoru isn't home so do it for him." But I didn't give up. I talked back to her, "Why don't we wait until Satoru comes back?" My mother said, "Don't talk back. Just do it." And she sounded really mad this time. But I said in a rough voice, "Okay, if I don't get to do my math homework, you have to make up for it." My mother stopped what she was doing and glared at me, saying, "Okay, since you talked back to me, you also have to clean the board at the bottom of the tub."

I didn't want my father to come home and scold me so I reluctantly went to the bath room. And I said, in a small voice that my mother in the kitchen couldn't hear, "I'll thumb my nose at you."

And then I took off the top of the tub and drained the water. The water goes out making a loud sound "swish." My blood pressure jumps up "whoosh."

When the water is still 15 centimeters deep the great flow slows down and loses its energy, going out bit by bit. It's going out about two or three centimeters a minute. Finally, taking about five minutes the water all went out.

The bottom of the tub was dirty. There was lots that was gooey and when you touch it, it feels like snot. Also there were long hairs piled up around the drain, about 30 centimeters long. It was sickeningly long hair, probably my mother's.

I tried to wash the dirt out with water but it didn't easily go away. "Okay, if that's the way it is, only Bath Magic Ring can help," I said in a louder voice than I meant to. From the kitchen my mother asked, "Tooru, you are shouting. What happened?" "Oh, nothing," I said cheerfully, as if I had forgotten what had happened just a while ago. Somehow I began to get a desire to work. "Okay, I am really going to clean it," I said and I squirted Bath Magic Ring into the tub "sss." And I rubbed the bath tub with a brush as hard as I could. There were little bubbles where I had brushed. It smelled good. It was a kind of smell that you would be happy to have even if your stomach was full. "Tooru, have you changed the bath water?" my mother said. I was in a good mood, but after she said that, my mood was destroyed. My mother said, as if she was in a good mood, "If you're through, hurry up and get done and I'll give you a snack." I thought, "With that tone of voice it's probably hotcakes and tea. I'd better finish quickly." But my back hurt. I worried that "if my back is bent at this age, what is going to happen when I get to be an old man?" so I stretched my back quickly before it would really become bent. I did it over and over. The pain went away after I concentrated on that exercise. "Ahhh," I sighed. My back was straightened and I felt relieved. I thought, "Okay, when my back gets straightened, I'll start again."

I pinched the hose so that the water would come out hard and when I turned on the faucet the water came out too hard and splashed my face. My face was cold with water so I took a bath towel from the closet next to the bath room and wiped my face desperately. Then I started cleaning again.

This time I pinched the tip of the hose after I turned the faucet on a little, so I would not make the same mistake. That way, I thought, the water would not splash my face. My guess was right and the water did not splash my face. And I washed away the bubbles in the bath tub. The bubbles which were stuck on the tub got piled up at the drain and didn't go out easily. I tried to wash them out with water but they wouldn't go out so I pushed them with my hand. Then the bubbles disappeared. So I put the bath tub top back and I turned on the faucet full force. The water made a loud whooshing noise and began to fill the tub quickly. It goes up four or five centimeters a minute. When the water begins to be deep it makes a smaller swishing noise, although a while ago it was making a very loud noise. However, the water pressure was the same as before.

When the water was about 60 centimeters from the bottom of the tub, I stopped it. It was so much cleaner than before I cleaned it. There was no dirt at the bottom and the water was clear and pretty.

I was more tired from today's bath cleaning than the bath cleaning I have done before. And I really felt good when the bath cleaning was over.[3]

The criticisms the teachers expressed about this piece reflected uncertainty about the boy's sincerity in writing as he did. "Stereotypical descriptions," "No obvious sense of self," "Flippant writing," and "Appears ecstatic with his skill" were some of their generalizations. They specified the overuse of phrases such as "a loud noise" and "a loud voice" as generic description and they questioned the sincerity of his concern over his rising blood pressure and bent back. Because the boy showed a flair for sensory description and a lively way of reporting conversation, it was not primarily his writing skill, but rather his intention in writing that was being called into question. He was thought to be too glib, too able to gloss over reality with a film of melodrama. Apparently the minute descriptions were not seen as overly detailed by these teachers, for they credited him with technical skill in regard to details. The problem they indicated was a lack of the kind of strong connection to reality that makes him want to write. The teachers seemed to be saying that, like cleaning the bath, the boy had the skill and could even enjoy the process, but lacked something in the way of inner motivation.

One teacher, however, sympathized with the discrepancy between this boy's self-expressiveness and the definitions the other teachers were using for sincerity, saying, "The gap is between the teacher's expectation and where the child really is. Children should be encouraged to write what they actually do, so that they won't be tempted to fill the gaps by adding moralizing endings." Indeed we sensed that this is a perennial problem, that children who have been told to write "as it really was" may sometimes anticipate teacher disapproval of the attitudes thus revealed. They are tempted to add a phony statement of insight or moralization to the writing. At the annual meeting of the national organization policy board in 1984, a similar question appeared on the agenda: "How are we going to overcome the expressions within and at the end of compositions that are insincere statements of determination and morality?" As it turned out, this particular issue was not directly addressed at the meeting. However, its inclusion on the agenda is indicative of an awareness that sincerity is easier to idealize than to actualize, especially in school writing, where assignment deadlines and misunderstandings about the goals of writing may make it hard for students to live up to such ideals.

In their drive for what we have been calling sincerity and authority, seikatsu educators stress to their students that they should simply base their writing on *jijitsu*, "as it really was." *Jijitsu* may be translated as "fact reality" and therefore can be contrasted with interpretive reality. The teacher, however, encourages children to write "how you felt at the time" and "what you thought at the time" as well as "what appeared before your eyes at the time." The boy who cleaned the bath seemed to follow those directions meticulously in recording the noises of the water and other physical descriptions. Perhaps his problem was that he attempted to interpret dramatically his own resistance to the chore, culminating in his sense of final achievement. In doing so, according to the teachers who criticized his writing, he went beyond the range of *jijitsu*. One of the biggest differences between seikatsu composition training and American writing education is that the budding of dramatic flair, which this boy showed, is often fostered in America, even when it seems a little phony, but is not encouraged in Japan, at least in the seikatsu classes we studied.

Kokubun recommends that a composition like the following should never be praised. This is an example of what he calls "generalized concept" writing, a type of writing that seikatsu training attempts to counter (Kokubun 1952:31):

AUTUMN

Autumn has come. A cool wind blows. The sky is blue and clear and we can see the pebbles at the bottom of the stream. In the mountains the chestnuts fall from the trees, and mushrooms sprout in the woods. The maples on Tenjin Mountain are beginning to change color and the singing of small birds sounds cheerful. It is an autumn that makes everyone feel healthy. When I get up in the morning and wash my face, the clear air penetrates my lungs. The cosmos flowers by the well are in full bloom. I will study hard, get lots of exercise, and develop a strong body. Autumn is a wonderful season.

Kokubun says that this is the sort of composition that is apt to come from a "straight A" sort of student and often appears as a prizewinning essay in a contest. If publicized and praised in class, other students will abandon their efforts to search out something real in their own lives and will begin to try to imitate this writing.

The self-actualization role in the seikatsu curriculum is an ambitious one. Theoretically it attempts to guide students into making an internal-external connection upon which their lives might rest. None of this is defined with great specificity, but what has been recognized are some of the barriers to that sort of idealistic linkage. Thus, the seikatsu teacher can patiently tolerate all of the inadequacies of "I saw the earthworm the earthworm Suzuki grabbed the earthworm" and appreciate the tsuzurikata, or connection-making, of the first grader who put her sense of awe into words. Yet the teacher may despair over fluency and dramatization in writing that overlooks *jijitsu* in quest of impressing an audience. This was often described as a "lack of self" but is a phenomenon that we sometimes refer to in English by the phrase "lack of voice."

When people write only from external motivation or knowingly create something other than what they actually experienced, their connection with reality becomes entangled in their reader consciousness. Their sincerity and authority can be questioned, so they must present their case with that possibility in mind. The validity of their writing is open to question by the reader. Whether seikatsu education is primarily language-arts training or oriented to self-actualization, seikatsu teachers attempt to separate the writer from reader issues, which might impinge upon the writer's sincerity and authority. Students are asked to write only from *jijitsu*—fact reality—until they are ready for advanced writing, which generally occurs beyond elementary grades. Teachers cull the problem cases from those they share in class. The writer's peers are generally expected to consider their classmate's writing with the assumption that it is written with sincerity and authority.

We asked Kamemura how teachers would deal with the following situation, which occurred in Mary's class in America a few years ago. A child unconsciously wrote from what must have been her image of reality rather than an actual memory. She wrote convincingly about her father's funeral and seemed to gain therapeutic benefits from the writing. Mary learned later, however, that the student had been less than a year old at the time of her father's death. Kamemura suggested that the girl may have written from *shinjitsu*, that is, from a truth that is "the substance of reality." From subsequent experiences, such as attending other funerals or hearing stories about her father's funeral, the girl had worked out for herself an interpretation of reality that was very important to her. Since she is still so young, he said, it may be that her *shinjitsu* should not be directly confronted by any *jijitsu* demands; but when she gets older, she will have to realize how it really was, perhaps by interviewing her mother to clarify for herself the actual situation.

CHAPTER **11** REALITY CONNECTION
AND WRITING

There is no lack of fantasy in the lives of children in Japan. As in America, they are exposed to an elaborate world of make-believe through reading and television. Yet writing a story by creating a plot around an animal family with human characteristics or by making up a monster tale is not included in the seikatsu curriculum for elementary-school children. If a child does write a fictional piece, the teachers told us, that is considered a special case, to be dealt with on an individual basis. If, for example, a fifth grader shows his teacher some fiction he has written at home, the teacher, in a completely accepting way, may help him work with the writing on a one-to-one basis. It is on the class assignment level that fiction writing is one of the last genres to be encouraged. Furthermore, if a youngster presents as a true personal narrative something that could not have happened, the akapen commentator may gently suggest that the child "wished" it could have been true.

Within the seikatsu framework the vital connection is the one writers make with their experience during the writing process. The words "I saw the earthworm the earthworm Suzuki grabbed the earthworm" are expected to do more for the writer than the reader. This first grader will be encouraged to be more scrupulous with attention to details, to sensory-emotional memory data, and to observational clarity because these things forge a stronger bond between her and reality. Such a bond is not considered possible for children in the process of writing fiction.

The value that seikatsu proponents claim for this training relates to some basic assumptions about the relationship of human beings to their world. Although Japan is a country of notable scientific achievements, scholars in many fields have observed that there is a traditional inclination to place particular value on the direct, intuitive perception of reality, rather than on the building of hypotheses.

The child who wrote about the earthworm had a connection to reality as soon as she saw that earthworm. According to the tenets of seikatsu philosophy, she had a more solid link after she wrote about the event; in creating a text, she grounded herself to reality. This stance on realism emerges as an underlying assumption in documents about seikatsu writing, namely, that linkages to reality occur directly in the course of everyone's experiences. This attitude differs from the notion of reality as something we conceptualize in terms of the hypotheses we develop (which, in turn, are created on the basis of experience). There seems to be a strong cultural basis in Japan for the belief that the reality that matters (though not the only one) is that which is directly attainable by means of perception and intuition. This notion of reality also entails valuing the concrete as opposed to the abstract. Although we can only speculate, it seems that a definition of reality as the sum of all that could potentially be experienced is a natural background for the seikatsu curriculum. If reality is intuitively available, children can connect directly into the reality system of life and solidify that connection through writing. If, instead, reality is something we comprehend by hypothesizing about it, then writing may need to be communicated and evaluated against other views in order to test the validity of each hypothesis. In other words, the hypothesis-creation outlook is more likely to result in reader-biased texts, in which the writing of a hypothesis is a preliminary step in making a thesis. The intuitive grasping of reality, however, does not rely upon further testing. Instead, reality connections are improved internally (that is what is called "being grounded in reality"), and writer-biased writing aids this process.

If the writer can have a straightforward experience of reality, this perception of reality can be appreciated, in turn, by a reader who encounters the experiencer-writer's text. Secondarily to the connection the writer made is a sharing of that perspective by the reader. That is another reason why the text should be detailed and truthful: when I read what you wrote, I have access to your connection to reality. Your piece of reality and mine add up to two pieces.

The issue of truth telling is important in this framework of reality connecting. It is also thought to be healthier psychologically and more appropriate to young children's cognitive levels of development. Until the later stages of seikatsu education, the student is encouraged to represent as accurately as possible, without improvisation, that segment of reality that is experience.

Since children in seikatsu training are not encouraged to write fiction, the reader is expected to take at face value what the writer has expressed in a text. The question is not the belief system of the reader as influenced by the text, but the connection made by the writer. Writers present the segment of reality that they have encountered. Their authority is that it has happened to them and is not a second-hand experience. They want to express it for no other reason than to express it. The writer's sincerity is this straightforward desire to share a segment of reality. It is not an issue if the reader has a piece of reality that seems to disprove the writer's. The two cannot refute each other if neither is a hypothesis; one piece of reality cannot be put against another in the same opposing way that hypotheses can.

To illustrate how this works, let us assume that the five blind men in the well-known tale of the five blind men and the elephant each present their piece of (elephant) reality without hypothesis: each one simply describes his connection to the elephant as he experiences it—rough and tubular, broad and flat, ropelike and short, and so on. Each one might appreciate the opportunity to express his portion of "elephantness" and would attempt to appreciate the others' perspectives as well. But there should be no argument among the five of them, for no one presented a hypothesis to be refuted or upheld. Each person only presented his own experience with "elephantness."

If, instead, reality is seen as being not directly attainable through intuition or perception, but must be postulated as a hypothesis on the basis of bits of evidence, the whole picture changes. Each of the blind men declares his hypothesis about the elephant and argues against the counterhypothesis of the others. Only to the extent that there is agreement, synthesis, or capitulation does the image of the elephant satisfy the rest of the group.

We will use the term *piece-of-reality approach* to characterize what may be the nature of realism in seikatsu writing. A model that can be contrasted to the piece-of-reality approach may be one articulated by George Kelly, a noted American psychologist, in whose view humankind is chipping away at the task of understanding the universe by setting up and testing hypotheses. According to Kelly, people create templates for themselves, which they fit over their experiences, and they use these templates, to the extent that they fit, to construe the world (Kelly 1955:89). When the text is one of realism, the reader tests the writer's hypothesis in the reader's own system of templates, perhaps to improve them and so construe more of reality. When the writer has written fiction, the reader looks for consistency in the hypothesis, for fiction writing can be seen essentially as hypothesis creation and development. One of the reasons that the composing of fiction is an advanced stage in the seikatsu sequence of development is that it is a cognitively complex task to create and maintain the elaborate network of hypotheses that are necessary to uphold the credibility of good fiction.

If a text were primarily a hypothesis, the reader's task would be to exercise comparative and contrastive judgment upon it in order to improve, ultimately, the reader's own hypotheses. That is why the text, in that sense, would be reader-biased prose. It would work upon the reader, if it were effective writing. The reader might choose to consider the writer's authority and sincerity as part of the evaluation the reader would make, but what must affect the reader most would be the validity that seemed to be contained in the hypothesis of the text itself. The reader has options of either countering the hypothesis in the name of "getting at the truth" or accepting the hypothesis in the name of "going along with the game," as one must do, for example, to enjoy *Alice in Wonderland*. On the other hand, in writer-biased prose, as defined in the seikatsu tradition with its reality-connecting function, to challenge the text is to challenge the writer's authority and sincerity, to imply that the writer has an ulterior motive directed toward influencing the reader or that the writer is not telling fully and correctly her own piece of reality.

Literature is, by definition, reader-biased writing. But to the extent that the intuitive view of reality is accepted in a culture, even reader-biased writing might reflect something of the piece-of-reality approach as well. One might expect a tradition of professional writing in Japan that simply presents the reader with the writer's perspective minus an apparent or implied hypothesis. Charles Grinnell Cleaver used a comparative study of Faulkner and Kawabata, among other pairings, in order to explore differences in American and Japanese popular imaginations. One of his points is that Faulkner's symbolism is more abstract and geometric (Cleaver 1978:145):

Suggestions about the world don't radiate naturally and inevitably from those arcs and circles; meanings must be lent to them. They therefore have a cerebral quality to them that differs from Kawabata's symbols. Kawabata's mountains and insects are not empty of idea, but idea seems less a separable or necessary part of what they signify.

Cleaver describes Faulkner's characters as constructs, representations of types, and notes that Faulkner wants to know the beginning, middle, and end of his characters, while Kawabata "wants to know the practical consequences of his characters' qualities, at given times, when they touch others" (p. 145). Kawabata's stance, in our terms, reflects a piece-of-reality approach—the moment can be presented in isolation from the past or the future. Rather than concerning the reader with how this segment of existence fits into the overall pattern of life, Kawabata concentrates on wringing from the minutiae of details some essence of momentary reality, as in this scene from *Snow Country*:

Each day, as the autumn grew colder, insects died on the floor of his room. Stiff-winged insects fell on their backs and were unable to get to their feet again. A bee walked a little and collapsed, walked a little and collapsed. It was a quiet death that came with the change of seasons. Looking closely, however, Shimamura could see that the legs and feelers were trembling in the struggle to live. For such a tiny death, the empty eight-mat room seemed enormous.[1]

Without going into the complexities of the issues involved, we can identify one small phenomenon of narrative writing that seems to relate organizational decisions to the piece-of-reality approach. Both professional and nonprofessional writers in Japan sometimes seem to cut away from a scene in the middle of it. The composition "Mulberry Gathering," presented in chapter 10, was a personally revealing account of being a second lieutenant without resolution of the problem. It ends abruptly: "It was getting dark and there was the noise of the river." The author seemed to use this almost unrelated sentence as a way to get off stage. The entire piece of writing is more reflective than teleological, so in order to get out of the spotlight, the writer turns the camera eye to some universal scene like the river. The alternative would have been to present some resolution or determination about the future, but if such did not occur, reality writing does not allow the boy that option. One of the difficulties with piece-of-reality presentations is that they do not necessarily have a sense of conclusion. Without hypothesis creation there is no framework to define the borders of some experiences. The boy, probably unconsciously, used a technique that was also employed by the adult whose writing we will discuss below.

The *Asahi Journal* is a weekly magazine devoted to what might be called "hard" news. A letter to the editor that appeared in the *Asahi Journal* for June 8, 1984, struck us as a typical example of piece-of-reality writing. Its presence in the company of letters about a French linguist-philosopher, housing for the elderly, and a recycling base for nuclear fuel made it all the more striking, for those letters contained clearly stated theses in contrast to this one:

My three year old son was to appear on the NHK television program "With My Mom." So one April day my wife, my oldest daughter, my son Yasuo and I went to the NHK studio in Shibuya.

Yasuo loves this program and always watched it with envy in his eyes for the children his age appearing on the program. So seeing his fondness for the program, my wife applied and got an invitation for him to appear.

Yasuo is a shy child so we were concerned whether or not he would play with the other children on the program. But we thought it would be nice if he got on television even a little bit. And we parents got kind of excited and bought him a new yellow outfit. We called our parents to tell them to be sure to watch the program and our neighbors sent us off with "Good luck."

Maybe Yasuo sensed our feelings for he began to get nervous as we got closer to Shibuya. When we were walking along the corridor to Studio 103 where they tape "With My Mom," Yasuo looked at my face as though he wanted to go back home. As expected then, Yasuo did not want to be part of the game and did not want to leave his seat in the spectators' part. There were several other children like that and some were crying. Those who were crying were ushered out of the studio by the personnel and their parents were obviously irritated. They were angry with their children who did not come up to their expectations. It was the same with us.

On the way home in the car Yasuo was asleep, exhausted. In his hand he carried a souvenir card and a balloon that he got from the studio usher. I said to my wife who was looking downhearted, "Yasuo was the only one who said, 'Thank you' for the balloon." My wife nodded, "Yeah."

White cherry blossoms, which had begun to bloom around the palace moat, were visible from the metropolitan highway.[2]

If we ignore the cultural attitude behind this letter, we may see it as unclear writing, with too many possible interpretations of the father's thesis. But he seemed to be putting the whole experience into the context of a universal concept of reality when he set it against the backdrop of the cherry blossoms.

Teachers whose students have an ethnic background that differs from their own, including teachers of English as a Second Language, need to consider any possible cultural dependency in their students' writing. Distinctive techniques may be recognized as having a cultural basis related to that group's world view. When the Japanese writer effects closure by means of reference to some universal imagery such as cherry blossoms or the sound of the river, it may give the text a poetic tone. This might seem incongruous if used with certain hypothesis-laden texts, but if the writing is a piece-of-reality text, that technique functions as a substitute for resolution.

CURRICULUM

CHAPTER **LESSON PLANNING**

Revision and Appreciation

"If you want to have a look at our visitors, get it over with now before we begin," Kazuo Takeda advised the third graders, and forty-two pairs of eyes turned toward us at the back of the classroom. Once their attention was redirected to their copies of a classmate's composition, they read along silently as the author stood and read his composition aloud.

THE GRANDFATHER WHO DIED

On the 15th of September my grandfather, who was about 68, died. I remember many things about Grandpa.

In the summer when I said, "Let's go to the swimming pool," he talked with Grandma for about five minutes and said, "Okay, let's go." When we got noisy because of our happiness he got mad and said, "Hurry up and get ready and get in the car."

When we got home about 5 o'clock after playing and swimming at the pool, Grandfather would drink milk and take a nap or watch television and read the paper. And, an hour later, we would have supper. We sat in the kitchen and Grandpa ate in the next room. Grandpa would raise his hands holding the bowl over his head and say Thank You in a small voice.

Grandpa's bedtime was usually around 10:30. In the morning he got up about 6:15, went to the bathroom, changed his clothes, watered the plants, and offered prayers for as much as 20 minutes. After that he went to his company carrying his lunch and his tools. When Grandpa was not home I was bored so I watched television and read comics.

Grandpa fixed big cars. Sometimes he would go around the neighborhood driving the cars.

In winter, because his company was close, Grandpa telephoned home and said, "Toyokazu and Akemi, get some bags and come here." So when we took the bags to him he put in tangerines someone gave him and he said, "Take them home and eat them."

In the spring about April Grandpa called me, "The fig tree has figs." When I said, "I want to eat them," Grandpa said, "They are too hard. When summer comes I'll let you eat them." And in the summer, as he promised, he gave me the figs. Grandpa asked me, "Are they sweet and delicious?" I said, "Yeah, sweet and delicious."

In the spring the next year, April 5th, we moved to Chiba. When we left Grandpa said, "Take this," and gave me 5000 yen.

One year and five months later, September 15th of last year, Grandpa died. And Grandpa's house became a lonely house and when I go to Grandma's house I remember Grandpa every time.[1]

This was an appreciation session, one of the culminating sessions for a composition unit. On each of the two previous days, another composition had been "appreciated." Each lesson was devoted entirely to one composition. Today it was Toyokazu's turn. After two or three such sessions, the class would move on to another unit, but other compositions are saved by the teacher for possible utilization later in the year.

At the conclusion of the reading, the teacher smiled broadly and reached for another set of copies on his desk. "That was the original draft," he announced. "Toyokazu has already revised this composition, and I have underlined all the revisions."

The teacher, a curriculum specialist in that school, had conferred with the boy personally, drawing out from him in conversation some of the additions he could use to clarify the writing. Most of these were details about time and location. The writer established the fact that he was writing primarily about events that had happened before he entered first grade, when the family lived with his grandparents. He had added details about the car repair business and his grandfather's religious customs. The paragraph with the most expansion was the following (additions underscored):

In the spring about April Grandpa, <u>standing by the fig tree at the house</u>, called me, "The fig tree has figs. <u>Come and see.</u>" <u>And when I went there running he showed me, "Figs have formed."</u> When I said, "I want to eat them," Grandpa said <u>smiling</u>, "They are too hard. <u>They'll get sweet and tender</u> when summer comes <u>and</u> I'll let you eat them." And in the summer, as he promised, he gave me the figs. <u>They were sweet and soft and even the parts that looked rotten were also delicious.</u> Grandpa asked me, "Are they sweet and delicious?" I said, "Yeah, sweet and delicious." <u>Grandpa grinned and said, "Swe-e-et, huh."</u>

After the class admired the additions, they categorized them according to the types of clarifications they made. Then the focus of the talk moved to the topic itself, grandfathers. After some discussion, most of the class seemed to concur with one boy who generalized that fathers and grandfathers both make promises, but that grandfathers have a better track record of keeping them.

This boy's school is unusual in that it has developed a schoolwide curricular policy to follow the seikatsu writing philosophy; it is rare that a school contains more than one or two teachers fully devoted to the seikatsu writing movement. Developmental steps expected in terms of writing ability are spelled out in a curriculum guide written by the teachers of this school.

The sequence of lessons in this composition unit was the pattern most typical for seikatsu writing classrooms: motivation giving, organizational planning, writing, revising or editing, appreciation. Usually one or more sessions would be devoted to each of these processes. In this school, the revision stage seemed to be emphasized more than in most seikatsu programs.

Although these teachers favored a very direct language-arts focus, many of the writer-biased attributes we have been describing are also apparent in their brand of seikatsu writing education. Writer bias can be noted in the ways teachers respond to students' writing and also in the sorts of responses they elicit from the classmates. In this instance, we noted evidence of writer bias in the ways in which the entire lesson reinforced the writer's insight about his grandfather. The textual discussion celebrated the writer's original experiences with his grandfather and applauded the writer's re-experiencing of that relationship through writing. Whether as a result of their training, the teacher's modeling, or some cultural attributes, Toyokazu's classmates were remarkably generous with the spotlight so that both the boy's experiencer-self and his writer-self were fully acknowledged. Then, when the classmates shared their own experiences and personal insights, they maintained the writer's topic, grandfathers, with the effect that even their general discussion was supportive of the author.

Motivation Raising and Organizational Planning for the Lower Primary Grades

On the same March day that we visited those third graders in their unit-concluding appreciation session, we watched a class of first-grade students beginning a new composition unit. The children were being primed to write about spring, the teacher told us, because modern children fail to fully recognize the rhythm of the seasons unless specific attention is called to the variety of changes that occur. The composition being used "to raise the desire to express oneself" was one that had been written by a child in the adjacent first grade:

This happened a little while ago. When my sister and I went out to play, we found a veronica flower. My sister said, "Oh, it's a veronica. Then spring is here, right?"

I said, "Let's take it to show Dad."

When I tried to pick it, it was hard to break off. I thought, "Even though it's only a flower, it's alive, eh."

I laughed. "Ho, ho, ho." My sister scolded me, "It's not something to laugh about." At last I did it. We went running home.

When we arrived at our apartment building, the flower was wither-
ing. My sister said, "We'd better go faster."
I said, "Ready? Go."[2]

As in most first grades in Japan, where children are eased into discipline very gingerly, this class was quite rambunctious. With such a high energy level directed in many directions other than the teacher's words, we were surprised at the quality of the students' responses. The teacher, Keiko Yamada, asked them, "Where can we find spring?" Their first answers were examples from nature, so the teacher made a list of these on the board. Then she asked them for indoor evidence that spring had come. An energetic youngster seated directly in front of us demonstrated excellent double focus. He managed to keep track of our note-taking by repeatedly walking back to our seats in apparent fascination over the fact that Mary was using romanized letters (English) and Chisato was using ideographs (Japanese). But between these visits he participated in the discussion long enough to explain that the goldfish at his house seem hungrier now that spring has come. We were surprised to hear first graders making observations of such subtle distinctions as the fact that their mothers did not bother to serve hot foods so often in warm weather, and that it was more frustrating to stay inside after supper now that the days were longer.

With answers coming in a steady stream, the teacher changed the activity to the filling out of seed cards. These the children drew from a supply they kept in envelopes in their desks. Each slip of paper, or "seed card," had spaces for the child's name, a topic, and a main idea: for example, after the child's name would be written "goldfish" and "hungrier now." As soon as it was filled in, the child would rush to the front with it so it could be taped onto a chart under one of the headings: nature, household or other. Some filled out several seed cards; about a third of the class did not finish any. The teacher read aloud some of the ideas that had been presented and suggested that everyone should think of an idea by the next day.

These first graders had accomplished the first two steps in the usual seikatsu writing sequence of lessons in a composition unit: motivation and organization. Older children would be expected to make more elaborate plans before writing, but first graders would be ready to write on the basis of their key idea from the seed card. Most of these first graders seemed to think spontaneously of a topic and a main idea directly after the theme was introduced by the model composition and the teacher revealed her interest in their spring experiences. The pre-writing stage was appropriately brief.

Motivation Raising and Organizational Planning for the Upper Intermediate Grades

In another school we followed a fifth-grade class through several days of organizational activity, guided by a teacher whose dynamic manner in the classroom held their attention to the task over several sessions. Masao Hino wanted to give his students practice in writing a composition based on a series of related events. The students were used to writing up a single incident that happened at "a certain time, a certain day." That is the typical kind of writing used in journals and in compositions for the first few grades in the seikatsu writing curriculum and will be described in detail in chapter 14.

As students followed on their copies, Hino read aloud an example of a composition with a time frame longer than a single event. It was by a girl in Tokyo and was a composition he had obtained through his association with other seikatsu writing teachers. He pointed out how the main idea was carried through description of a series of events. Then he asked the students to identify how such a composition differs from description of a single event. As the students floundered over that problem, he asked why the choice of using such a series might be more significant, more expressive of the main point, than describing a single, well-detailed episode alone. Synthesizing their responses, he led them to the conclusion that the effect may be stronger when the writer links events that have a common thread and also that the writing both requires and sustains a greater energy.

This was to be their task as well: to write a composition that would encompass a period of time and would link a series of related happenings or perceptions. To illustrate how varied the time span might be, he wrote on the board: one year, a month, a week, three days. Students were asked to think of contexts for each of these in which the time might be considered "a long time." One boy indicated his comprehension of the point by joking that the model composition Hino had read might be called "a certain month, a certain time." Indeed, the writing did have the cohesiveness of "a certain time" specificity, while describing a series of events occurring over a period of weeks. Hino's direction to his students was to "find for yourselves a topic about which you have been carrying a sustained energy." This theme was to govern their search for subject matter over the next few days. He also discussed the requirement that there be personal involvement and that it be something about which the student had already done a great deal of thinking. In this way, he indicated that the subject matter for this composition already existed in the student's life. The prewriting process would be to discover a reality connection that had already been made. The students' task was not to create a connection, but to search for something already present, though possibly submerged, in their conscious experience.

We were reminded of Ken Macrorie's *Searching Writing*, a book that describes what he calls the "I-Search" paper (see Macrorie 1980). To select a topic for the basically primary research of an I-Search paper, Macrorie recommends that writers delve for a topic that they genuinely want to explore. Both the I-Search paper and the writing experience in Hino's classroom entail an elaborate process of introspection to find the best topic.

One boy in Hino's fifth grade asked if he could write about the bombing of Hiroshima. Hino agreed, speculating that this might seem that he was yielding on his requirement that there be personal involvement. He explained that this was an exceptional situation, however, because Hino knew that the boy had recently read a book that had so moved him that his involvement with the subject, though not direct, could be said to be personal.

In a class meeting at the end of that day, and over lessons on each of the following two days, students listed possible topics for themselves. In some sense these were brainstorming sessions, in that students were encouraged to broaden their possibilities, not narrow them down. Unlike items exploding out of most brainstorming sessions, however, these ideas came forth with some deliberation. Students mentioned only topics that they were actually evaluating for themselves in terms of personal commitment. After each session Hino made copies of the lists, including the name of the person who was considering each possibility. He also organized the lists by category, such as Playing and Sports, Nature, Siblings, and so forth. Each time the students were given a new list, they were challenged to come up with potential topics in some of the categories other than ones in which their previous topics appeared, using those listed by others to trigger seed ideas from their own experiences and perceptions.

In the lesson in which the final decision was made, each student filled out a planning sheet, which specified the following: topic (one or two words, as in a brief title); expanded topic (explanatory version of the topic or title, incorporating feelings or personal involvement); subtitles (one for each potential part of the composition); contents (memoranda to indicate the events, feelings, etc., for each corresponding subtitle). The teacher used one boy's topic, the heavy snow of that winter, to show the class how the planning sheet should be used. Students contributed examples of their own snow experiences for listing on the board, and the teacher demonstrated ways to link their randomly organized, specific events into generalizations about snow. The rest of the period was given over to the filling out of the planning sheets with individualized assistance by the teacher.

If we count the class meeting among the prewriting sessions, four periods were devoted to preparation before the day of actual writing. One session was set up as a motivation-raising activity, two were given over to topic choosing, and one was organizational planning of the text itself. This is more prewriting than teachers generally require of fifth graders in American schools. Again, the prolonged grappling for an appropriate topic may be seen as an attribute of writer bias. As in the I-Search paper, this writer bias often serves the reader as well because the writing tends to carry the author's imprint, or voice, through to the reader. In selecting a topic, both the I-Search paper and seikatsu writing require that writers go through the topic-choice process on their own behalf, to find what Macrorie describes as an itch that you just have to scratch.

Donald Murray describes writing as a series of texts. The first is the *text of intent,* written mentally or by means of notes. This, he says, is destroyed by the *text of reality,* the actual text, which, in turn, may be attacked by the *text of response,* which occurs to us when we reread and revise (see Murray 1984). The students in Hino's class spent four periods working on the text of intent, two on the text of reality, and one on the text of response. Furthermore, since the rather complex assignment called for a topic "about which you have already done a great deal of thinking," it might be claimed that the students' experience through the large part of the school year already past had led them to anticipate their topic on some level even before the unit began. Since the writing appeared to be quite cohesive, in spite of little time spent on post-writing reorganization, we may assume that the lengthy rehearsal is an effective launchpad for powerful writing.

We have already mentioned, in connection with journal writing, that one of the effects of writing regularly is to bring inner speech to the conscious level more readily. Students in a *seikatsu* classroom may begin to lead something of a prewriting existence, much as professional writers seem to do.

Whole-Group Timetable and Editing

In Japan, pupils are accustomed to whole-group assignments that also include whole-group timetables. Most of the seikatsu writing teachers we questioned indicated that, unlike journal entries, compositions produced for a writing unit are primarily written in school. The weekly schedule is often rearranged to provide two back-to-back writing periods on a certain day for a total of about ninety minutes. Although students may sometimes be allowed to complete the writing as homework, the actual text is often produced and submitted on a whole-class timetable and rather soon after writing begins. A single session for editing and making any revisions follows the day of actual writing; then the piece is submitted to the teacher. Of course, this typical sequence has numerous variations.

Although the composition unit ends with a few appreciation sessions as soon as the teacher has read the papers, it does not mean that redrafting is automatically out of the question. Some students redraft compositions to which the teacher and/or class has already responded. Many teachers promote voluntary rewriting, especially when the topic seems to be particularly relevant to that child. This is similar to some of the practices Graves and Calkins recommend after watching young writers at work. Rewriting something meaningful is a logical extension of writing it in the first place. That makes sense. It is the rewriting of a piece that did not jell in the first place that makes little sense. If we are taking a reader-biased outlook, we may demand useless or untimely revision. With a writer bias, it becomes evident which instances of cycling back through the same topic are natural extensions of the original composing processes.

In spite of the existence of possibilities for reworking a piece of writing, however, it is more typical for a seikatsu writer to produce a new composition on an old topic than to make extensive organizational revisions in a single composition. On the basis of both journal entries and compositions written during a unit, seikatsu teachers readily shift roles in the direction of individual guidance to encourage a student to continue to pursue a significant topic outside of class or in a future writing unit. In terms of whole-class expectations, the revision session as the fourth stage of a composition unit is often time largely devoted to careful editing.

The series of appreciation sessions at the end of a writing unit is not necessarily the last view of the compositions from that unit. A piece written early in the year might be used months later to introduce a theme or to demonstrate something the teacher hoped others might be ready to emulate. The use of model compositions that were actually produced by children known to the class or by students of the teacher's seikatsu colleagues makes for a positive recycling process whereby a class spirals upward through the developmental levels discussed in chapter 14.

CHAPTER **13** POETRY

AUTUMN DISCOVERED

Lying on a patch of grass
Kusu kusu it is, a good feeling,
Fuwa fuwa it is, a warm feeling,
When I put my ear to the ground
There was the cry of an insect.
Soon this insect
Will be dead, won't it?
The sun made me squint.
Even so,
The wind was cool.[1]

Kusu kusu and *fuwa fuwa* are onomatopoeic expressions; the first is the boy's original creation but seems to give a prickly fresh image to native speakers of Japanese, for whom onomatopoeia is an important part of sensory language. *Fuwa fuwa* is a standard way to describe something soft and billowy.

In a circle group-meeting, we asked this child's teacher, Hiroshi Tsuzaki, what his aim was in having his fourth graders write poetry. "I wanted to have the children discover something about reality that they had not discovered before they attempted to compose the poem," he replied. He also mentioned that the writer of "Autumn Discovered" had had a rather low standing, both socially and academically, but that he had changed for the better over the course of many writing experiences. This was his first poem.

Poetry occupies a special place in seikatsu writing and has been a part of the curriculum since the beginning. According to Kokubun, poetry is art and, as such, differs from the autobiographical narration that makes up the bulk of seikatsu writing. Children's compositions and journal entries are not to be considered or treated as literature, he says, but poetry is a legitimate extension into the field of literary creation.

In order to locate the function of poetry writing in the overall scheme of seikatsu writing methodology, let us consider how poetic writing differs from other forms of written expression. Children in seikatsu writing classrooms learn first to write in prose about an event of "a certain day, a certain time," deepening their contact with reality by heightening sensory awareness. The cure for superficiality or over-generalization in prose writing is to strive to be more explicit. Revision, when it occurs, usually consists of the *addition* of details. Poetry, on the other hand, allows the writer to experiment with *subtraction* as a form of revision. Significantly, revision is considered vital to the writing of poetry, in sharp contrast to the lack of stress on revision in the composition of seikatsu prose.

Time, in poetry, is often somewhat universal, as for example in "Autumn Discovered," when a very specific occurrence represents an entire season because the poet chose *not* to document the experience in terms of "a certain day, a certain time." In his journal or in a composition, the writer would probably have followed his training to indicate where, when, and how all this came about. The effect of a documented account of this incident would be quite different: the teacher or other commentator might say, "I'm glad this youngster realized this bit of insight." The effect of writing that omits specification of the location or time can be to universalize the image and open it to others in a more vicarious way. Any one of us might have the same feelings of *kusu kusu* and *fuwa fuwa* when we lie on a patch of dry grass in the warm sun with a cool wind blowing and hear a tiny, soon-to-die insect's cry. "Ah, yes," we say to ourselves, "that's the way it is in autumn."

From expressive to poetic writing, there is the writer-reader relationship that Britton, after Harding, labels a co-spectatorship. In seikatsu writing, when the intimacy of the child-writer and the teacher–akapen-wielder broadens to include even an unknown audience, there is a branching toward literature. In poetry, language is formed deliberately to create an effect. An image may hinge upon a word painstakingly chosen. A child may even feel compelled to create a word like *kusu kusu* because of an image which must be expressed in just the right way.

Sueyoshi Eguchi is a teacher known for his success and wisdom regarding seikatsu poetry. Both Eguchi and Britton describe poetry in terms of the way the image is transmitted to the reader. Britton talks about "heightening or intensifying the *implicit*" (1975b:13); Eguchi says that the unique function and value of poetry education is for children to go through the difficulty of isolating material that is suitable for poems and expressing it so that it may be grasped directly. Compositions, he says, "are intellectual and extend through time via paragraphs, whereas poems are intensive, emotional and direct" (1968:45).

Japanese appreciation of the implicit is evident in many forms of art, including haiku poetry (which, incidentally, is not typically part of Japanese schoolchildren's writing experiences in either seikatsu or non-seikatsu writing classes, being considered too restrictive for children; the type of poetry taught widely in Japan is free verse). In discussing literature with an allusion to painting, Cleaver refers to the concept of *yohaku*, 'the remaining white,' meaning that part of the canvas left unpainted (1976:134), and says that Japanese writers typically allow the reader's imagination to fill in much of the *yohaku*. Seikatsu training in prose writing encourages students to leave very little of the *yohaku*; teachers want students to delve deeply, so they ask them to fill in all possible details in writing their journal entries and compositions. But poetry writing is an antidote to such a requirement and provides another dimension by letting the student articulate more precisely some quality of experience without documenting the event itself. According to Eguchi, the belaboring of expression involved in choosing words for a poem not only sharpens language skills, but also nurtures children's "emotional, intuitive, imaginative, and observational qualities" precisely because they have to find ways to concentrate them into such concise expression.

Since seikatsu poems are always free verse, the form is not bound to any sort of formulae in terms of meter, rhyme, verse, and the like. Eguchi further recommends not teaching form at all, but emphasizing instead the writing of strong emotions with whatever moving expressions children sense they need. This, he says, will lead to crystallized expressions, which will naturally divide into short lines (Eguchi 1968:246). The guidance he would have teachers provide is to point out that after each line the blank space contains unexpressed words, not written because they would be redundant. It is the combination of expressed words with blank spaces that carries sentiment, that makes a poem a poem. Students thus come to appreciate also what is unsaid, but implicit. As a demonstration of this, Eguchi added to one of his third grader's poems the "redundant" parts that he postulates a reader might imagine, but that the writer did not write because the expressed part makes them clear. Eguchi's additions are shown in parentheses (1968:248):

KURUHARA-SAN

Finally	*(recovering from an illness, Kuruhara,)*
You came today	*(over a week later)*
After a long absence.	*(You must have had a bad time.)*
Oh,	*(Even though you've recovered, still . . .)*
But you look pale.	*(You had a high fever. Please take care not to get sick again. See, everyone, she doesn't look strong, so let's be careful with her.)*[2]

Most children's poems are far less haiku-like than this. But Eguchi's explanation of poetry as a crystallization of imagery is perhaps reminiscent of the fact that the Japanese culture is the source of haiku and that haiku societies continue to flourish there, even though not as a medium for children's writing.

Poetry is writing that says only what you most want to say. Seikatsu prose is studied in class by having students debate what the writer most wanted to express. But, in writing a poem, it is the poet who isolates the *kandoo* (heart surge) for the reader. Furthermore, the poem must contain one and only one such "heart surge."

While praising the following poem as a major achievement for a first grader, Shigeo Noguchi, who is the mentor of the study group made up of circle-group leaders of the Tokyo area, observed that the poem is actually made up of two heart surges instead of one. He suggests that the child should have broken it off after the seventh line:

CRICKET
A cricket
Came flying to my nose
"Kiri kiri
Kiri kiri,"
It sang.
Because of its beautiful song
I kept lying there.
My nose began to feel ticklish.
I sat up
It landed on my tummy
So holding it gently
I let it go
Beside a stone.[3]

After an outing with some fourth graders, their teacher, Ryuuhoo Tsubata, discussed the following journal entry description with one of his students:

After we arrived in Matsuguchi, following the teacher's instructions carefully, we started gathering mountain herbs. We went to a low rising slope to gather the herbs. I tried to get an udo [an asparagus-like wild plant] *by pulling it up. And the* udo *came out suddenly, making me tumble down the slope.*

"Sumie, what part did you most want to tell me?"
"Hmmm, let me see. The part that the plant came out and I fell."
"Well, then, would you rewrite this, telling just about that portion?"
Sumie produced the following poem:

GATHERING WILD HERBS
Trying to get an udo
I pulled
The udo *came up*
And I fell down the slope
But
Down to its white root part
It came out quite neatly.[4]

Eguchi describes the difficulties children may have in distinguishing poetry from prose. Sometimes what they identify as prose seems more like poetry to their teacher, and often the reverse occurs. Eguchi says that even first graders, by the end of the year, can begin to sense the difference intuitively if they read and hear many examples of prose and poetry (excluding haiku and other non-free poems). As they listen to a piece of writing, Eguchi uses four categories: (1) This is a poem, isn't it? (2) This is like a poem, isn't it? (3) This is like a composition, isn't it? and (4) This is a composition, isn't it? In this way students come to realize that there are different ways to grasp material, and this realization helps them learn to express themselves differently according to their intentions for the reader.

Eguchi cautions against overstressing the poetry/prose distinctions. He says that much of first graders' writing is not clearly prose or poetry. It is only the teacher's desire to know that demands an answer. Of the following example, Eguchi questions: "Is this a poem or prose? I think it is a poem, but if someone argues that it is prose, I'll accept that."

CAT

A cat sleeps on the roof
I don't know how he got there
Today I finally found out
He got up by the persimmon tree in the back.[5]

Whether consciously or instinctively, this first-grade boy put the first two lines in present tense and the last two in past tense. It would be risky to teach this technique, for the child might become artificially locked into a technique. Instead, just as in having children write everyday experiences into narrative form, the writing rings true because it is based upon reality and is not contrived.

First graders in Japan frequently write about the common childhood experience of not getting to the bathroom in time:

ACCIDENT

I had to go wee-wee
There was a bathroom but
I didn't tell the teacher
Everyone was eating lunch
I ate my lunch
The wee-wee began to come
I said, "Hah"
I tried to hold it but
It kept coming
I turned pale
I lifted myself up
My seat cushion was wet
I thought "Oh, no"
Just then my cup fell
Water spilled
It puddled with the wee-wee under my chair
"What happened under your chair?"
My friend asked.
I
"Water got spilled"
Made a lie.[6]

Eguchi has devised some methods with which he guides the various stages of poetry writing. One way to help children discover that they have something to write, when they complain that they have not, says Eguchi, is to remind them:

You must have had some experiences that surprised you, or times recently when something struck you as strange so you told your parents or friends about it. Let's write those words. (p. 133)

Have you complained about anything, laughed about anything, cried about something recently? No one has not done one of these in the past week or so; write it so the scene comes through. (p. 143)

He advises allowing children to write as if they were speaking, using direct address such as "Say, Mom" or "By the way, Teacher" and including the Japanese speech particles that convey the speaker's attitudinal state and inner feelings (see Uyeno 1971). The first step of poetry education is to let children write with the natural expressions they utter when they are moved by their feelings. Then these expressions may be removed to see if what remains contains the same feeling. The following poem contains speech patterns that the child was encouraged to remove, resulting in a poem that contains only those words not underlined below:

HOMEWORK
Teacher Minowa,
You give lots of homework, <u>don't you</u>?
How about just once
Why don't you give us
"Eat ice cream" homework, <u>I wonder</u>?[7]

Another example of revision by subtraction is the following poem, in which the second grader later erased the speech pattern portions (the underlined phrases):

BULB
<u>*Say, Mother,*</u>
In science class, <u>you see</u>,
Teacher, with a knife, <u>right</u>,
Cut a tulip bulb straight through the center.
Inside, the circling white lines
Were like an onion, <u>really</u>,
He said it was a red tulip, <u>right</u>?
But <u>I tell you</u> it was not red inside.
<u>*Strange, huh!*</u>[8]

The key to discovering material for the contents of a poem, Eguchi says, is to help children realize that there have been things in their everyday lives that they feel compelled to talk about because they cannot forget them. One second grader wrote five times about a small quarrel between his parents. Every time the teacher said, "Let's write a poem," the boy explored the same topic. Here is one version of his poem:

PARENTS' QUARREL

When Papa was sick
Mama brought medicine
Papa said
"I don't need it."
Mama said
"You have to take it."
Papa said
"I don't want it."
Then Mama cried.
She cried, "Een, een."
Mama said to me
"Go downstairs."
I said, "Umm,"
And went downstairs quietly.
I felt
Pity for Mama
Pity for Papa
It was raining outside.[9]

Originally, Eguchi says, there was another line: "So I couldn't play outside." Therefore, the last line's feeling of loneliness may not have been a conscious effort. Eguchi wanted to help the boy express his own sadness and loneliness, so he showed him how that fact could be carried in the concluding image of the rain.

Besides writing about an experience that may have had a momentary impact, poetry writing can be used to have students focus upon something that has sustained their interest over time. Things pass by on television and disappear before children have a chance to ponder about them, Eguchi observes (p. 137), so writing poetry has an important place in modern society. For an example of writing from extended thinking, he includes the following descriptive poem by a fifth-grade boy:

COCKROACH

We say of detestable people that they are like cockroaches.
We say cockroaches are representative of insect pests.
Pity the cockroach
Detested by everyone, beaten by brooms,
Doused with pesticides, he dies.
Cockroach
Has the same kind of life as butterflies and dragonflies.
One gets protected, one gets killed.
The cockroach himself doesn't know
He's doing anything deserving of this.
He runs fast, he flies a bit,

He's just trying to live.
People cut short this life, kill it.
Why did God create such an insect?[10]

Without reference to meter, versification, or rhyme patterns, the poems of seikatsu writing, like the prose, tend to reverberate in accordance with the emotional substance they reflect. To be effective, this emotional substance is better expressed by allusion than by direct expression. It is as if the students are being guided by the adage "Show, don't tell," which we hear from many quarters in this country (usually in terms of writing prose). Upon the suggestion of an akapen comment, one student substituted the lines "Only the drip of the faucet / Drip, drip / The sound of the dripping is all I hear" for her original statement, "I am lonely," in a poem about coming home to an empty house.

Onomatopoeia is basic to Japanese descriptive language (and hard to translate into English with its relative paucity of such words). The following poem rests so strongly upon the combination of personification and the enlivening use of onomatopoeia that the relative absence of similes and metaphor is not particularly obvious.

PAPER PLANE

Yura yura [*implies gliding movement*]
Fuwa fuwa [*implies billowing softness*]
Rides on the airflow
Not to fall
Not to fall
Praying that, it goes on crossing
The clear, blue sky without a sound,
One meter, two meters,
Kuru kuru
Kuru Kuru [*implies a spinning movement*]
The wind goes by, giving way for it,
Yura yura
Fuwa fuwa
A little while longer, give me freedom.
A little while longer, give me a dream.[11]

The following two poems, by a second grader and a ninth grader respectively, utilize the opportunities poetry gives them to do a little editorializing:

THE TEACHER'S YAWN

Ah, the teacher yawned!
What a big yawn!
The lips painted red with lipstick
Rippling outward, k'waan [*bell reverberations*].
Right above the nostrils
A wrinkle appears.
The eyes behind the glasses
Are thin and creased.

Oh, how unattractive!
Teacher,
Really, it doesn't look good,
Your usual nice face is completely gone.[12]

WHY IS STUDY BORING?
When teachers get mad
Their talk flashes straight at us
But when it comes to lessons
Their speech brings darkness before our eyes
Why is that?
Even during lessons
Why can't their talk come flashing at us?
All teachers are the same
And that's why classes are boring.[13]

We noticed that gentle, and not so gentle, ribbing of the teacher seemed to be a popular theme in poems presented by teachers for discussion in circle groups. Similarly, sometimes compositions functioned as a forum for children's reproof of the teacher or school. But there may be a difference, for a child, between using prose and poetry to make a point. When children acquire the necessary skills of abstraction, the entire scope of seikatsu writing can be used consciously to project the sense of self in terms of relationships, society, or mankind. Poetry, however, may provide an especially accessible, albeit sometimes unconscious, outlet for such self-projection from the very beginning:

KINDERGARTEN WAS BETTER
Hurry up. I want to eat lunch.
Are there no snacks?
Are there no blocks?
The slide is broken.
There is no jungle gym.
Kindergarten was better.[14]

The classic poetry of seikatsu writing is contained within a collection of poems written by Matsusaburo Oozeki, a sixth-grade boy, during the 1937–38 school year when his teacher was Michio Sagawa. These were published first in 1951 and are often used in seikatsu classrooms as models. Sagawa said of the relationship between teacher and student:

The teacher must discover history in the child's life. Then, the teacher must have the child become aware of it. Education exists there. Viewed thus, what children come up with is a joint authorship of the teacher, the child, and life. (1951:62–63)

The famous poem from which Oozeki's book of poems takes its name goes like this:

YAMAIMO [MOUNTAIN TUBER—A BIG, KNOBBY, EDIBLE PLANT]

From the bottom of the earth, dug up with so much toil
I pry out a huge yamaimo
Coming up, coming up
A gigantic yamaimo
In between its thick, gnarled fingers
The earth is still grasped firmly
The heavy, massive yamaimo.
Hey, holding it this way and looking at it
Each and every one, a farmer's hand,
Dirt-encrusted and stained,
With hairy and bony knuckles,
Awkward, but full of strength
Without mistake, it is a farmer's hand.
It is my pa's hand, exactly.
I wonder if my hands will become like this.[15]

And again from that collection:

MIMIZU [EARTHWORM]

Hey, you,
Like having no head and no tail,
Like having no eyes, nor hands and feet,
When harassed, you only twitch around,
A not-at-all frightening thing.
All day long crawling under the ground
Plowing through the soil
Eating only rotten things
Living by doing only that.
Even if a hundred, two hundred, years pass,
You are the same naked thing
Unable to become anything more,
Stupid and pitiful thing,
You are the same as the farmers,
Yes, you are one of us.[16]

In the following poem, Oozeki, who incidentally did not live through World War II, combined his training as a detailed observer with personal empathy for the horse, even though there was nothing he could do to remedy the situation. In this way, the poem may illustrate the traditional idealism in the seikatsu movement that writing may serve to give children a voice, even in situations in which they have no other.

UMA [HORSE]

Hey-up, you, hey-up, come on.
Whap, whap,
Whap, whap,
The cartman, raising a thick rope,
Beats the neck of the resisting horse.

The horse jerks back his head
With wild tossing of his mane,
He snaps back his neck, flailing and twisting.
The cartman leaps up and strikes him
Where the veins bulge like thick tree roots.

Whap, whap,
Whap, whap.

The horse and the cart, chock full of charcoal bins,
Are being driven backwards into the storage barn.
The horse, planting his hind legs firmly,
Kicking up dust with his forelegs,
No matter how often beaten,
No matter how often shouted at, he would not go backwards.
Hey-up, you, come on.
Whap, whap,
Whap, whap,
The sound pierces the air
Coming from the jerking neck.
How could I be made to go backwards?
Forward, I would go.
I'd go no matter how heavy the burden.
But, backward,
No matter how often beaten,
No matter how often shouted at,
Not one step will I retreat.
Yes, yes, not to go backward.
Is it not unreasonable, unjust?

I was crying within myself.
Whap, whap.
Everytime he gets hit, he jerks back.
Baring his red gums, the horse is angry.
The hind legs dig sharply into the ground,
The chest muscles bunch up into knots.
Without a cry, he is fighting.

Win, win, horse,
I was crying out in my heart.

Whap, whap.

But the cartman finally gives up.
Ceasing the beating, he pulls forward,
The cart rolls easily,
And, circling around, goes right into the barn.

I was relieved.

I wanted to cry out, Hooray.

The northwind came sweeping down,
Blowing dried radish leaves hanging in the barn,
Rattling and almost tearing them off.[17]

CHAPTER **14** STEPS ONE THROUGH THREE

May 26. Today when I climbed the wooden climbing poles bare-foot, Eiji-kun said, "Do you have to climb them barefoot?" "Yeah," I said and I did it again.[1]

Tadashi wrote his journal entry in what seikatsu teachers define as step one writing, a basic level of abstraction for written communication. Step one writing typically retells the event chronologically, generally in the past tense.

Five levels of abstraction have been defined as being an expected developmental sequence in the seikatsu writing curriculum. These progressions were defined formally as a proposal by the national association policy board members in 1965 (as described in chapter 6), and were made the official curriculum by the membership in 1982. The five steps describe a progression, beginning with the straightforward personal narrative of a single event (step one) and then explanatory-style writing with an actual or implied time span that is longer (step two). Step three is a combining of steps one and two, usually to achieve generalization with concrete examples. Step four is the writing of a research paper, and step five incorporates all other types of writing, including fiction and formal exposition.

A concomitant shifting toward reader-biased writing also takes place so that, while the writer-biased personal narration of step one sometimes includes speechlike prose, the reader-biased fifth step involves the coordination of selfhood into the intricacies of formal written communication.

Although we found no evidence of research or communication between Japan and the West regarding this theory, we noticed many coincidental and analogous relationships between the five steps of seikatsu and the type of writing education that has been advocated by such researchers as Britton and Moffett. Moffett recognized progressions that could be formed into a matrix of development by charting an ascending level of abstraction onto a grid with an ever-widening rhetorical distance from the writer (or speaker) to the audience. "Rhetorical distance and abstractive altitude furnish coordinates of distance and abstraction by which we can map the universe of discourse," Moffett writes (1983:155).

As we have already indicated, seikatsu writing evolves from a relationship with a most immediate audience and only gradually expands to include readers widely separated from the writer in time and space. In the seikatsu curriculum, the levels of increasing abstraction are defined as the five steps.

One coincidence between these five steps and Moffett's matrix is that both relate levels of abstraction to an aspectual/modal hierarchy of verbal constructions. As Moffett defines the first step, we record what is going on at the time by telling *what is happening* as immediate perception. At a point later in time we can report *what happened*. At a more abstract level, we may generalize from these happenings to make explanations of *what happens* (sometimes, usually, always, etc.). Then, at a more abstract level, we could choose to project from these generalizations a theory of *what can or will happen* (see Moffett 1983 for explication of these levels).

Except for quoted speech or thought, *what is happening* is used particularly for scene setting. In a letter we may say, "I'm writing this from a beach on the Riviera," or in writing a script, "The maid is dusting the piano." *What is happening* is a way of recording an immediate perception or setting. Takajiroo Imai (1961:33), speaking of the seikatsu writing curriculum, recognizes description in the present tense as a foundation for narration, so he recommends an exercise of asking students to deliberately write about a past event in the present tense, as if it were still happening before their eyes. In this day of television instant replays and slow-motion photography, we can often mechanically re-view *what happened,* but exercises such as this indicate to students that writing makes the same demands on their memory systems. By means of the marvel of human memory, events can be replayed until the scene stands out clearly from the background of the writer's total life.

Generally, though, present-tense reporting is limited to on-the-spot descriptions, as in announcing a horse race. The instant the action is completed, past tense is the natural, formal way to report it. Since writing is normally done after the fact, the first step in the seikatsu curriculum sequence is the writing of personal narratives in past tense.

Hino had been a first-grade teacher the year before we observed him in the fifth-grade setting. He had written a journal article describing how he gave his first graders practice in turning their on-the-spot perceptions into descriptive reporting by making pancakes for them. He had slowed and dramatized each step, asking the children to write what they saw. We might presume four activities in this task, capitalizing on Vygotsky's notion of inner and outer operations: (1) they perceived his actions; (2) their thoughts percolated through inner speech; (3) their inner speech took on aspects of external language; (4) they wrote down some version of this interplay. Vygotsky says that there is a constant interaction between outer and inner operations with "no sharp division between inner and external behavior, and each influences the other" (1962:47). In Hino's exercise, the students' writing was a transcription of the shiftings between perception, inner speech (or *what is happening*), and reporting, often by shifting into the past tense. Here is one child's description of the beginning of the pancake-making action:

When Mr. Hino finished looking into the classroom, smiling through the window, he opened the door and, holding up a strange looking bundle, he looked up at the ceiling. He walked in steppity step and put it down on the desk plop.[2]

By freezing the action from time to time, Hino allowed the children time to make an immediate search through short-term memory, to verbalize, and to organize the verbal patterns into description.

According to Vygotsky, writing builds upon "barely emerging, rudimentary processes" when instruction in writing begins (p. 100). Written language demands conscious work because the syntax is quite different from inner speech, implying a translation process. A game like Hino's pancake-making activity (with the built-in reward of eating the pancakes) helps children practice the facilities necessary in learning to write.

After we returned to America, Mary tried the same cooking demonstration—writing activity with her fifth graders, making potato latkes for Hannukah. She found that, according to the various students' understanding of their task, some wrote in the present progressive mode and some translated their perceptions into narrative description with the past tense. In either case, students produced descriptive writing that included far more elaboration than had been customary in other writing, even though they were rushing to record their observations during the relatively short periods in which the action was frozen. We realized that one of the objectives of such exercises is to train writers to bring more of their perceptions to the surface as a resource for writing.

Step one, the personal narrative, is not only the beginning stage of writing for young children, but it is also the fundamental form of writing for students of all grade levels. Seikatsu teachers require it of their students of any age including high school, whenever they feel that the writer needs to make the most solid connection between self and writing.

Macrorie's I-Search paper, referred to in chapter 12, capitalizes on self-connection and the natural organization of temporal sequence as means for helping students produce a research paper. Graves has realized the advantages of personal narration as an easy genre because of its natural chronology and because the writer can use actual memories as a resource during writing (Graves 1983:155). So also seikatsu writing teachers have found personal narration easiest for reality connection through writing.

Step two in the seikatsu sequence goes beyond narration into explanation or generalization. Like Moffett's *what happens*, it incorporates present-tense writing in the generalization of happenings into statements of permanent, habitual, or typical conditions.

. . . My house is a bakery. Moreover, it is a bakery for homemade bread. It's not like other bakery stores where someone brings bread

by truck. . . . Even when there are no special orders Mother has to get up at 4 A.M. to start the dough. Dough is the basic material of bread. . . . "Oh, it's been a hectic day," she often sighs. Sometimes I massage her back for her. . . . [3]

This particular composition was written in Hino's class by a fifth-grade girl who happened to have gone beyond step two writing into step three. Had she written entirely in step two fashion, the entire piece might have consisted completely of such explanatory description as the excerpts above, probably using only the present tense. The constraints of the five steps, however, are meant only to guide the teacher in terms of whole-class curricular decisions and expectations. They are not intended to stifle the students. Teachers are not surprised when first graders generalize, or even mix explanation into narration. Writers of any age do in writing what they do in speech. The five steps are for the teachers' systemization of curriculum, rather than a lockstep developmental sequence that children will, or should, automatically follow. As indicated in chapter 6, the steps were developed in an effort to provide writing education the kind of logical framework that makes it both a language-arts discipline and a tool for encouraging self-actualization.

Yasue introduced her topic with a dialogue in which her mother complained to her, "Tomorrow I'll be getting up at 2 A.M. . . ." After a short narrative beginning, Yasue followed with an explanatory section in which she described life in a bakery-home. Then she picked up the thread of the opening conversation and concluded with a narrative related to that specific day. This alternation of explanation and narration is step three writing. Since Yasue happened to write in that fashion, the teacher could introduce the technique to the rest of the class by using her writing as a model. Had he not felt that others were ready to be made aware of the types of transition Yasue did, he might not have presented her writing to the class, even though he could still reflect her accomplishment to her individually by means of his response to her writing.

Making asides of explanation in the course of a narrative is a naturally occurring variation of straightforward retelling. As audience awareness develops, children take the reader's needs into account and incorporate necessary explanation. In schools in which there is a continuity of seikatsu writing teachers, it would seem likely that students could be made conscious of all three steps by the end of the intermediate grades. At the same time, there are seikatsu writing teachers who do not particularly adhere to these progressions, or who use them only as a very broad guideline for themselves, adding their own conceptions of developmental sequence. Seikatsu teachers of the Ena model, for example, do not utilize the five-step curricular plan. Their emphasis on writing for self and social development calls for a "form follows function" philosophy that precludes such a formal sequence.

In the five-step plan, step four is the formal theme or research paper and may be delayed until either junior high or high school. Step five, which basically includes whatever other writing the student needs to learn, such as essays, exposition, or fiction, is left for formal presentation in late high school or in college. However, as examination pressures continue to take precedence in the Japanese higher grades, steps four and five remain relatively uncharted territory in seikatsu writing at present.

We leave further discussion of steps four and five to the next chapter; here we look more closely at the first three steps.

The First Step

The phrase associated with the first step is "a certain day, a certain time." One of the suggestions teachers make to primary-school-age children is to begin a composition or journal entry by telling when the event took place. It is not that they have to specify a particular calendar or clock reference. "A certain day, a certain time" can also be indicated in relation to the daily routine. Children usually localize the time by saying something like "This happened when I was on my way home from school yesterday," or "During clean-up today. . . ." By predetermining, through seeking "what remains in your mind/heart," what it is that they most want to express, students know approximately what part of the day or of the daily routine to use as an opening. Once they have written down the time reference, all that remains is to follow the chronological sequence of remembered perceptions and observations.

The effectiveness of this "certain day, certain time" opening helps avoid the syndrome Graves calls "bed-to-bed" writing (1983:156), where children enumerate events from sunup to sundown without regard for their significance to the story. This same tendency had been noted by teachers in Japan; Kokubun lamented: "Once you get to bed everything comes to an end, but of course you have to have supper first. . . ." (1952:23). For Kokubun the correction of this syndrome is part of breaking what he calls the "generalized concept" type of writing and is, in fact, a fundamental challenge for the seikatsu curriculum. The stronger the reality connection, the more likely students will focus their writing precisely. Routinely beginning with a time or daily-life reference may not hook the reader's attention, but it seems to lock the writer on target.

Soon after the children become comfortable with an opening that establishes the time, they may be asked to do the same for location. The phrase used by teachers who specifically advise students in this way (not all do so) is to write about "a certain day, a certain time, a certain place." In spite of this extension, first-step writing continues to carry the nickname of its more common association, "a certain day, a certain time."

The essence of first-step writing is the journal entry. For students who have gotten into the journal-writing habit, it is not difficult to move into a more consciously structured first-step composition. They may even base it upon a journal entry, in which case the journal was a prewriting activity for the composition. And, without having to capture a reluctant reader's attention, writers usually write a lead and a concluding sentence that brackets the memory for themselves. With topic choice aided by the journal-writing habit as well as actual entries, and without the danger of audience apathy, much of the fear is removed from the writing process. By the time the teacher asks for a composition, journal writing has already taught the child "If that's what writing is, I can do it."

With chronological sequence to follow, children can concentrate on expressing all that they saw, heard, felt, and thought "just as it was at the time." Keiichi Takura (1985:16) says he praised a particular sentence in the following journal entry in front of the class because he wanted the writer's classmates to recognize how meticulously the boy had taken himself back through the sequence of perception:

I was reading a book in the evening and my mother called me from downstairs. "Shin, come downstairs." So I said, "What?" and came downstairs. Mother was putting something red on plates. I went to look at them. They were strawberries. She said, "These strawberries came from our own garden." I took them to the table and ate them.[4]

Although at the time of writing he knew that it was strawberries on the plate, this third grader was able to retell the event in the sequence of sensory perception. Tamiya describes the importance of training that leads a child to make such careful distinctions:

To express the self accurately requires the grasping of the objective surroundings. The more it becomes clear how to position oneself in the context of reality, the more objective the expression of the self becomes.[5]

This third grader successfully negotiated a time transfer in his mind to reconstruct the experience of recognizing the strawberries. Since seikatsu tsuzurikata is not a product-oriented curriculum, teachers must note such development in the writer rather than ranking compositions according to some external norm. Seikatsu compositions can be evaluated in terms of their potential value as models for others, but personal and expressive growth are individual matters. Takura says of the boy who wrote about the strawberries that he began to be more confident and assertive along with his success in writing.

One of the basic skills required in step one writing is detailed observation. This is similar to Mary's father's discovery as an amateur photographer of wildflowers that he could often observe more through the camera lens because of the way the viewfinder isolates the object. The memory search a child goes through for step one may result in seeing more by looking at less.

Children of seikatsu teachers are constantly enjoined to remember concretely just what it was that they saw, heard, or felt at the time. This brings to mind another analogy, a parallel that might exist between step one writing and drawing. Betty Edwards, the author of *Drawing on the Right Side of the Brain*, advises people who want to draw better to practice looking at the subject matter as an artist does. Instead of saying to yourself, "The back of the chair is rounded," she recommends letting the right side of the brain perceive where and how the chair-ness meets the non–chair-ness. She claims that people who draw well, in realistic art, do so because they do not let preconceptions interfere with what is immediately present to be seen. Without any apparent discussion about right and left sides of the brain, seikatsu teachers seem to strike a similar chord when they persist in requesting that students observe carefully and write precisely "as it was."

According to Kokubun, children in the primary grades "cannot be expected to write in detail unless they can express it with a sense of 'I' to support it" (Kokubun 1952:119). When a child writes about tomatoes growing on a vine, saying, "They were touching each other and just like a mother and a child,"[6] her description is the recording of a personal association. In spite of the fact that writing inevitably entails a certain amount of detachment by the child because representing a situation in writing is more abstract than conversing about it, her anticipation of a personal reader made the job easier. She opened by addressing the teacher directly and used a Japanese sentence particle that gives the effect of "Hey."

One of the marks of writer-biased education is that the value that accrues to the process, the reality connection, is realized as readily in a beginner's activity as in a professional's. Therefore, although steps two and three may be cognitively more demanding for the writer, the products cannot be ranked on that basis—that is, the writing is not necessarily more valuable at a higher step.

The Second Step

When teachers begin to notice definite signs of reader awareness, they may consider it time to introduce step two for the class as a whole. Writers' awareness of a reader, as we have noted, has been kept at bay so that they could become solidly grounded in their own connections to reality. For the most part, reader responses were designed to highlight what the writer seemed to want to express. Nevertheless, the teacher's responses, the class appreciation sessions, and maturation itself all play natural roles in fostering a sense of audience. When students become aware of the need to clarify their narratives appropriately for the intended audience, the teacher broadens the concept of writing to incorporate longer time periods, sequences of events, and writing that is strictly explanatory. Undoubtedly many of the students have already begun to make generalizations and explanations in their narrative accounts before the teacher begins to make whole-class assignments of step two writing. By saving some such compositions, and others written by colleagues' students, the teacher has models with which the children can identify.

Whereas first-step writing is about "a certain day, a certain time, a certain place," second-step is "a long time, a fairly long time." Step one is a single event, distinct from what always happens, but step two includes things the writer has repeatedly or constantly experienced, thought about, or had feelings about. There are several kinds of writing that come under the heading "a long time, a fairly long time." One type is similar to step one writing, except that several related activities are described instead of just one. This has the effect of explanation or generalization, even if not overtly stated. Chronological order often provides the structure, just as in the writing of a single event. Another type of step two writing is primarily explanatory and may be written exclusively in the present tense.

Whether the thread that connects the parts of step two writing is an overtly stated theme such as "This winter's heavy snow has greatly affected my daily life," or is the recitation of a series of related events that portray some progression of experience, or is purely descriptive writing, the decisions required of the writer are much more complex than in step one writing. When the teacher moves the class into step two writing, the most obvious curricular change is to expand the time allowed for organizational planning. Motivation and topic choice remain important, but the student may also need to work out the framework of the whole piece.

The following composition by a fifth grader has a clearly stated theme, which is carried out in the text and reiterated at the end. It seems to be an unusually well-organized example of step two writing. As is often the case, the explanatory style description and the generalizations are written exclusively in the present tense.

RUNNING A PUBLIC BATH

My father's oldest brother runs a public bath. And that bath is called "Horikiri-Yu" and since it is located in the same neighborhood as my house, I often go there to help out. It might look like running a public bath is an easy job, just sitting at the desk and collecting money, but really it is not.

Every day they start cleaning from about 10 in the morning. My aunt does the women's section and for the men's section, a man who is a relative comes to clean. To begin they put a cleaning machine in the changing rooms, then they wipe them down with wet cloths. This washing is the hardest work in the whole cleaning. This is because you have to do it barefoot; at the beginning the water is warm but as you keep scrubbing the floor with the cloths, the water gets cold and in the winter you get frostbite on your hands and feet. In addition, the section you have to scrub is wide so you get a backache. When you are through with this scrubbing, you clean the windows, the babies' changing table, and the lockers and you throw the trash out and sweep the entrance. And then, the second older brother of my father, who lives nearby, spreads something like powdered soap into the bathtub and scrubs with some kind of power scrubber. Then he sprays it with disinfectant. They do thorough cleaning like this every day because cleanliness is most important in a public bath, they say.

Besides these things, as part of the job for a public bath there is the important job of heating the water. That work begins around 1:30 P.M. First they put some water in the bathtub, then they put fuel in the tank and turn on the switch. Then automatically the fire goes on. When it gets to 42 or 43 degrees centigrade they put this hot water into the tub. Heating the water is the part that requires fire. There are about five large extinguishers and they are set so that, at the time of an earthquake, the fire is automatically extinguished. When they heat the water there is a roaring sound that reminds me of a crematorium. So I don't like that sound.

Then at four the bath opens. At first my uncle takes over the desk. He does this after opening the entrance and putting up the cloth doorway covering. When a customer comes, he says "Welcome" and takes the money. The fee is 230 yen for adults and 110 yen for elementary school children and 60 yen for younger children. Inside the bath they sell such things as shampoo, rinse, soap, razors, juice and ice cream.

They say that the customers they don't like are the drunks. Drunks take long baths and when they come out they sometimes are shouting, "I'm dizzy, I'm dizzy," disturbing other customers.

Other than drunks, the other customers they don't like are people who use too much hot water to wash with and people who hand them a 10,000 yen bill without apologizing. They say that when they get handed a 10,000 yen bill suddenly, they have trouble keeping change at hand.

Also there are people who talk a lot in a public bath, for example, in a gossiping, chatty way. "Say, it's scary nowadays, isn't it, so many suicides," or "My child is such a picky eater and it is such a nuisance," thus enjoying their talk, particularly the women, they say. The little kids are just like little kids, washing their doll's hair and playing with water pistols. People talking in the bath echo resoundingly and it's like listening to the news.

When you run a public bath you cannot straightforwardly tell customers off or warn them, because you have to give good service. My aunt and uncle say that they want as many customers as possible coming to their business.

So neither my aunt nor uncle uses rough language and when a customer says, "I can't get hot water" they communicate right away through the intercom to the uncle at the heating unit.

Like this, running a public bath requires a lot of work in the areas people do not notice and takes a lot of care in attending to the customers. It's hard work, I think.[7]

We did not observe her class, but if this author had filled out a planning sheet in an organization lesson such as described about Hino's class in the previous chapter, her expanded topic might have been "the little-known work of running a public bath such as my uncle's." Her subtitles might have been "cleaning, heating water, fees and sales, problem customers, and customers' behavior." Any of the information she had acquired through her association with her relatives' business might have been written into a past-tense, concrete example; this girl seems well enough acquainted with her topic to have concrete stories to tell. In this writing, however, she maintained the explanatory style throughout. The chronological sequence of the daily routine provided the order for most of her categories and made the reading easy to follow. When we consider the processes involved in arriving at so cohesive a product, it becomes apparent that the cognitive demands of step two writing are very great. It would be rare to find a child accomplishing this below fourth grade and common to find junior high school students who still did not handle the complexities well.

The theme "Introduction of a Family Member" is often used to encourage step two writing. It seemed significant that nine- and ten-year-olds of both sexes in Japan write readily on the subject "Mother and Me," whereas many American students of that age might balk at such a task. The social value of family and school relationships is important to the personal-development aims of seikatsu writing, so assignments are often stated in terms of writing about family, friends, and teachers. Furthermore, the subject of interpersonal relationships lends itself either to the format of a series of related events or to explanation, both step two types of writing.

The Third Step

The author of the public bath account maintained the present tense throughout as a way of generalizing and explaining. If she had written a narrative account of some specific event or series of events at her uncle's public bath, she would probably have used the present tense to make some explanatory asides that she thought a reader needed for clarification about the context. Such explanations are an acknowledgment of the audience. Even the purely explanatory style she did use could have been interrupted by means of tense shifts to include narrative examples that would further illustrate her points.

The composition discussed earlier in this chapter, in which the girl introduced readers to her mother's bakery business and also dramatized life in that context with a specific incident, is an example of appropriate step three writing. Instead of enclosing the explanation between the opening conversational bit and the continuing narration, she could have chosen to do the opposite. In such a case, the specific incident would have been in the middle, between an opening generalization and a conclusion that elaborated on the main point. Since the explanatory material was in the present tense, the verb tense readily indicated the point at which the writer had turned to face the audience or split her vision between the audience and the story.

Some lessons we saw at the fifth-grade level involved students marking verbs to examine the use of tense. In Japanese the final verb determines the tense of the entire sentence and is easily located, usually at the end of the sentence. By marking sentence-final verbs and watching for any shifts, the organizational structure of the writing can sometimes be traced. Children who are skillful at such transitions have an effective tool for writing.

Step three is the stage of writing development in which the writer skillfully manipulates tense as a fundamental discourse strategy. Most students who attain step three effectiveness will do so by interweaving chunks of writing according to their intentions, as in the following example, in which the present tense marks explanation and the writer's perceptions, but the past tense is used for narration and background:

RABBIT SLAUGHTERER

"Clack, clack, clack."

"Hello," came the rasping voice from the kitchen door. This is the same man who comes to our house every year, the slaughterer of rabbits, whose job it is to kill rabbits for meat.

He seems to be in a hurry and tells my grandfather he'd better stop one of these days or he'll get revenge from the spirit of the rabbits. My grandfather says, "Don't be stupid. Unless we kill rabbits we won't have meat for New Year's," as though he was talking about some vegetables.

I had been raising rabbits for three years. When there was no grass, I took them to the rice paddy and let them play. Sometimes I stole carrots from the kitchen for them. Why do we have to kill the rabbits now? I began to feel that my heart was going to burst, not so much out of pity for the rabbits as against the cruelty of man.

I closed my eyes and could only see the rabbit boxes. The rabbit slaughterer and my grandfather apparently felt differently and I could sense even from the sight of their backs a kind of excitement.

The man was skillful and quick and soon the rabbits became a pile of meat. Our supper was rabbit and I realized that I had come to share the mind of the rabbit slaughterer and my grandfather because I thought it was delicious. I wondered why I could eat it so easily while I detested the rabbits' killing so violently.

I decided to forget this whole event because it was too tragic for the rabbits and too cruel of human beings, but I'm not going to raise rabbits anymore.[8]

If successfully done, as in this case, tense shifting enables the reader to shift focus as well, and seems to draw the reader into the scene. If unsuccessfully done, the reader experiences great uneasiness.

Although children seem to acquire this ability automatically as they mature, seikatsu teachers who teach the steps formally delay introducing step three in class until the developmental level of the students is clearly equal to the task, in the upper elementary grades or later.

In the following composition, a fifth-grade boy seemed to be experiencing confusion related to use of verb tense when he tried to write about events covering a long period of time. The changes in perspective are not always clear. (He had spent several years in America, so his problems may be attributed to re-entry difficulty with using Japanese again in schoolwork.)

ABOUT FISHING DURING THE LAST THREE YEARS

It started three years ago when my father went fishing at Imba Lake.

The fish he got first was a crucian carp about 10 centimeters long. I think that fishing is fun whether you can get fish or not. It is because it is satisfying just to be able to fish.

My father's company is near the ocean so on Sundays I often accompanied him in order to go fishing. I say to my father, "How about if you fish too sometimes?"

But there are times also that I don't like. That is when my father gets the big ones and I get only small ones. Since then I did some research in secret so my father would not find out until we went fishing again. So one Sunday I said, "Which of us do you think will get the biggest one?" After only a short time passed I felt a pull. I thought, "It may be a big one." "I may be about to win," I thought. But when I pulled it up, it was small. I said, "Darn!" and put more bait on the hook. It looks like my father got one. Because my father said, "It's big," I thought, "Oh, it's already over." As I expected, I ended up losing.

When I was reading a book on fishing, there was a way of fishing called lure fishing. Thinking, "If I do this, maybe I can win," I made a lure-fishing contest at Orochi Pond.

What is called a lure is a thing that looks like a small fish or a frog.

Because we went there in June, I thought we could get fish right away but we couldn't. It became evening. I got a pull. I pulled it up quickly. It was a fish called a black bass, about 38 centimeters. I was just so happy I could hardly sleep that night.

Although I have been able to win every time when we did lure fishing, all the other times I end up losing.

These days we don't go fishing at all. I am thinking that we should go when spring break comes.[9]

Manipulation of verb tense can be seen as manipulation by the writer of the writer-reader relationship; sometimes it is a matter of refining the angle of perspective from which the writer presents the event, and at other times it effects a change in the directness with which the writer addresses the reader.

Teachers use the same strategy to become co-spectators with their young writers through responses in the margins. The use of the present tense, including the present progressive, gives a sense of immediacy to words: "Here you are clearly recalling exactly what the fish smelled like at the time," or even, "Here you are listening carefully to the night sounds." The teacher steps into the writer's shoes and describes the writer's accomplishments as if they were ongoing. This is often done in terms of sensory observations. We might expect the teacher to have said, "I see that you remembered clearly how your mother's voice sounded and what her facial expression was." At times teachers do write in that mode, but there is an intimacy that occurs when these observations are expressed instead in the present progressive.

It is such an artful maneuver to interweave tenses consciously that we cannot imagine how this delicate a skill can be taught by means of rules, but the technique can be modeled. Consider the following excerpt from a composition discussed by Hitoshi Nakanishi in a seikatsu journal article. Present-tense verbs are underlined here, as in the journal article's version.

PULLING UP TOBACCO PLANTS

*. . . I walked right behind Mom stepping in her footprints up to
the upper farm. Some of the tobacco stems <u>are</u> standing upright
and some <u>are</u> bent to the ground. I started from the roadside edge.
When I <u>pull</u> one holding the lower part of the stem, it <u>comes</u> right
up with roots full of dumpling-like chunks of dirt. It <u>is</u> very heavy. I
thought, "It is because of the rain yesterday. Well, it is not going to
be an easy task." While I was thinking things like that, Mom had
already pulled as many as five. Mom <u>is</u> knocking them against the
row ridge. It <u>does</u> not look like an easy task for her.*

*When I was trying to pull the second one, she said, "Taka-chan,
try pulling them from the opposite angle to the way they are growing." I tried it just the way Mom told me and it came out very easily. I asked her, "How can I get the dirt off easier?" She told me,
"You hold the top of the plant, you see, and beat it against the
ground." I did as Mom said. It <u>comes</u> off very easily.*

*When I got a little carried away, raising it over my head to beat it
down, the dirt showered down on my head and bounced off. It
went down my back through my collar. Because it <u>is</u> wet it <u>feels</u>
cold. Holding the back of my shirt away from my body and jump-
ing up and down, I <u>try</u> to shake it out but it <u>does</u> not come out
because of the sweat. I thought, "I don't care," but then Mom said,
"You can get the dirt off by hitting the plants against the tobacco
plants that are still standing." So I did it and it was a lot easier. I
thought that Mom does know a lot. I began to get into the spirit of
doing it. I <u>look</u> around and already half of the plants have been
pulled. . . .* [10]

In the composition above, the boy often utilized the present tense
when reporting perceptions: "stems are standing . . . are bent" or "is
wet . . . feels cold." Some uses of the present tense are in cases of
descriptions that fit into the category of kinesthetic perception: "is very
heavy" and "comes off easily." The technique is a way of attaining
immediacy with the event on the writer's part and communicating the
sensory data to the reader. The problem is how to accomplish this
without becoming so mechanical about tense as to destroy the ex-
pressively natural qualities of a text.

As we might expect, such writing is difficult to achieve in long stretches
of text. It is even more difficult to teach; instead of specific instruction
in this special kind of step three writing, some teachers use exercises
to indirectly promote students' flexibility in use of tense.

One of the exercises recommended is the advice given by Imai,
which we have already mentioned: having students write a past event
in the present tense, as if making a sketch using words to capture
ongoing perceptions (even though the perceptions are actually only
memories). Another exercise for this is recommended by Tanaka
(1984:93), in which students are asked to roll a sheet of paper into a
tube and look through it to isolate a small bit of their surroundings,
or to close their eyes for meditative listening. Then they write what

they saw or heard in detail, using the present progressive or the simple present tense.

These exercises may be conducive to some step three style writing, but also seem fitting as training for any step. The demands in seikatsu writing for sensory acuity begin with step one and continue to enlarge. This is related to the fact that even as reader-consciousness emerges the writer-self *cum* experiencer-self remains the basic element of importance.

A question remains in our minds as to how extensive a curricular place seikatsu teachers are giving to variations of step three writing. But it does seem to us that a logical progression from learning to write in the genre of steps one and two is to become able to combine the two effectively.

A high school seikatsu teacher, Eiko Kouda, told us that launching step one writing is all that she needs to do for the first three steps, because students with mature language skills automatically move readily into steps two and three.

CHAPTER **15** STEPS FOUR AND FIVE

In March of 1982, when the five developmental steps that had been proposed in 1965 were made official policy by the national board of the seikatsu teachers' organization, step four was characterized as follows (cf. Nihon Sakubun no Kai 1984:87):

At this level the writer should be able to organize materials including that which is new to the writer, making suppositions, predictions, or opinions about the material, and organizing these clearly. Step four writing is based upon the second step, developing it further by heightening the generalizations and abstractions. This is the foundation for academic papers, essays, etc., for the upper grades in elementary school and above.

According to Kokubun (1984a), students should be advised at this level to utilize information gleaned from questioning neighbors and relatives about the past, or from published resources and lectures, incorporating both their reactions to what they learn and their own generalizations in terms of, for example, "this village" or "in Japan."

Step four resembles step two in the sense that students attempt to relate their inner feelings and thoughts to facts, expressing personal generalizations. But it exists as a separate step because there is another level of abstraction to consider. At this more advanced level, students utilize secondary resources more widely, reporting not just what occurred to them at the time of perceiving or acquiring the information, but also projecting from it some sort of thesis.

In the same official statement, step five was characterized in the following way (p. 88):

At this level, children and young people should be able to utilize all the abilities and methods of expression acquired through previous steps so that the written products may impress the reader to be highly communicative, persuasive, and/or moving. It is not so much a step as a culmination of all the preceding steps.

The ways in which steps four and five are defined and characterized may give the impression that they are but a natural extension of steps one to three. An interesting point to note, however, is that in seikatsu literature the flood of guidelines and discussion that pour forth to elucidate the pedagogy of steps one to three dwindles to a trickle when it comes to steps four and five. The guidelines that exist seem tentative and futuristic. One obvious reason for this is the fact that examination pressures exert a narrowing influence upon education above the elementary-school level in Japan and diminish the actualization of this part of the curriculum. Another often-stated reason is the fact that, although teachers commonly stay with the same class for two years in grade school and some follow a class along for more than a year in secondary school, there is not enough continuity with any given group of students to develop all the steps fully. Only in the rare schools where seikatsu writing is practiced throughout the grades could the entire five-step sequence be fully explored. But the contrast between the first three and the last two steps seems too great to be explained away in terms of those external factors.

Kokubun (1984a:96) admits that, in looking through the 1983 anthology of children's writings compiled by *Nihon Sakubun no Kai*, he found no writings that fully met the specifications of step four writing. However, he comments that certain fragments of some texts exhibit characteristics anticipated for such writing. Before describing our own speculations about the critical differences between the first three and the last two steps, we will present one such example which, according to Kokubun, has budding elements of step four writing contained within it.

This piece, "Grandmother's House and the Goemon Bathtub," was written by a sixth-grade girl in December 1982 in Goro Kamemura's class. (Kamemura, when we visited his class in February 1984, was teaching first graders, following them that April into second grade; but, as is common in Japan, he often alternates several years of teaching in the primary grades with upper-level teaching.)

The composition is very long, so we will present only some of the representative parts. The girl begins her narrative by describing a visit to her grandmother's house and continues with a description of the house structure and surroundings of that historic mansion from the mid-1800s. When she begins to describe the bath area, the writer skillfully moves into explanation with some generalization, in the following way:

This bath area has a glass entry door and when you enter there is a wooden wall on one side and on the left facing the garden is a glass window. Outside of the window is a chimney with a one meter high concrete foundation, and the rest, about 15 centimeters in width, goes up beyond the roof.

The bathtub placed here is a rare goemon bathtub. It is the same type of gigantic iron kettle which was used to execute that most notorious thief in Japanese history, Goemon Ishikawa, by boiling him to death. The bathtub is my favorite item out of everything in my grandmother's home.

The diameter of the tub is about 150 centimeters and it is made of iron about 15 centimeters thick. When you get into it, you step onto a round wooden platform, about 50 centimeters across, called the floating cover. It goes down under your weight. This we need because the kettle is heated directly so you would get burned if you touched the iron itself. To avoid that, you step onto the wooden board, but, if you don't get onto the center, maintaining good balance, the board might tip you off. . . .

Under the tub there is about 60 centimeters dug out and outside the concrete frame that supports the tub is a section about one cubic meter in which you can burn wood, fallen leaves, tree branches, or anything. So, when the bath water gets cold, if you have someone burn something a little, it gets heated right away. When it gets too hot, you cool it by fresh water, but at that time, there is no faucet so you get water from a pipe in the wooden wall by asking someone to turn it on in the kitchen. In olden times people carried water from the well in the kitchen by buckets. But it was so much trouble that Grandfather put this pipe through so well water could be directed to the bath area. That well is not used any more, so the water comes into the pipe by a hose from the faucet in the kitchen. . . .

Nowadays with gas and water plumbing there are a lot more conveniences, but they still maintain this bathtub which embodies many family memories. That is one of the reasons I love this goemon bathtub. Whenever I go to Grandmother's house, I always take a bath in this tub. . . .

With a goemon tub, the entire kettle gets heated and the heat comes from all directions so your body gets warmed in a very wholesome way. Taking a bath I look around through the thin cracks of the wooden boards in the wall. The smoke comes in from outside. The wooden boards and the ceiling have a deep black shine from the soot. And it tells you that it has been here from long ago. Taking a bath smelling that smoke makes my heart peaceful. . . .

My grandmother is now 84 years old. She has a little trouble with her legs and walks slowly because of a numbness in her legs. But otherwise she is really healthy. When Grandmother sees me and smiles, her crease-ridden face breaks up and her gentle, thin eyes become even thinner. Her skin is pale and creased with many wrinkles, but she has warm hands.

My grandfather is already dead. Born into the household of the shoya [a mayorial family of feudal times], he worked as the village mayor. Up until the 1920s many people worked for him in the silkworm egg-producing business. After that time too, there were people cultivating his rice fields and farmlands and this house was always bustling. . . . After the war things like that disappeared with the changes of the world and with land reform. So Grandmother told me in a nostalgic tone.

After Grandfather died, they stopped raising even cows and chickens. But I hope that they always keep the goemon bath which embodies so many memories. And I hope that Grandmother will live a long life.[1]

It is in the sections in which the girl notes the changing times and the realization of the historical importance of things like the antique bathtub that Kokubun recognizes the budding elements of generalization and abstraction characteristic of the fourth step. The author relates her experiences to her general knowledge, perhaps gained in social studies, and utilizes the resources of her father and grandmother to get information upon which she can draw conclusions. At the same time, Kokubun notes, by not stopping at description and explanation, but skillfully incorporating also her own inner feelings, the girl shows an ability that approaches literature at some points.

As far as the delineation of the five-step curriculum is concerned, however, a surprising lack of concerted effort on steps four and five still remains. It seems uncharacteristic of the proponents of the movement to leave the description of these steps and the recommendations on methodology so nebulous. We believe that there are significant reasons as to why steps four and five have not been fully realized. A plausible explanation is that these two last steps, although natural extensions of the language-arts curriculum starting with step one, carry with them elements somewhat foreign to the cultural ethos in which the seikatsu movement is embedded.

With step four, the notion of thesis building is introduced, which inevitably raises the issue of writing that creates and supports a hypothesis. This makes step four a radical departure from steps one to three in at least two important aspects. One is the question of audience. In step four it becomes critical that the readership extend to the general public; a good thesis must rest upon its intrinsic merits, whoever the reader. The other concerns the function of language. In thesis building, the writer uses language to create a world of its own logic. To cross from the first three steps to step four is to cross from the domain where language is used to make connections with a piece of reality to the domain where language is used to underwrite a hypothesis.

This is not the way seikatsu writing theorists themselves define the transition from earlier steps to step four. But this explanation is in accord with the long-standing claim (e.g., Kokubun 1952, Sasai 1981) that the seikatsu writing movement is firmly rooted in the indigenous cultural heritage of Japan.

A predilection for the specific and concrete at the expense of the abstract and general has long been noted by Japanologists, if mostly in speculative and anecdotal terms, as a significant attribute of the Japanese cultural pattern. According to Hajime Nakamura, the "Japanese way of thinking habitually avoids summations of separate facts into broad statements about whole categories of things" (1967:191–92). He shows how a number of abstract concepts developed by Indian and Chinese Buddhist logicians took on empiricistic shading in the Buddhism that took root in Japan. He explains that Japanese people are not inclined to present universal concepts as absolutes but rather "are not usually content until they have presented a set of particular instances or individual cases pertaining to universal propositions" (p. 187). Prescott Winter, speaking of the system of knowledge in eighteenth-century Japan, strikes a similar note: "Since knowledge could not rely on a small number of theoretical statements, each needing validation in one or more proofs, the alternative was to continue to amass details. . . . Whereas European knowledge soon became very 'paradigmatic,' Japanese knowledge remained 'plethoric,' with consequences that only became apparent in the nineteenth century when the two cultures confronted one another" (1982:420).

The preoccupation with the specific and concrete seems to be very much of a factor even in Japan today. A columnist for a leading newspaper, *Asahi Shimbun* (May 10, 1984), described his impressions of a "Japan–France Cultural Summit" held in May 1984 in Japan, expressing continuing wonderment at how different the two cultures are:

This does not mean that both sides do not agree on issues. It is only that they differ at the level of fundamental attitude and perception about things in general. . . . Comments by the French gravitate toward theory and abstraction. They begin their statements with definitions of words. . . . On the other hand, comments by the Japanese are in general based upon the concrete and individual experience.

We identified this same distinction in chapter 11 in terms of two distinct types of conceptual framework—the "piece of reality" model and the "language of hypothesis" model. We may surmise that steps one through three, constructed in the "piece of reality" model, are truly Japanese in their emphasis on the individual recognition of the concrete and immediate as being the essential reality of life. It is this reality to which the seikatsu proponents want children to become grounded through their experience of writing about the actual events of their everyday life. The fact that step four abstractions may be more of a hurdle than present seikatsu writing methodology has managed to overcome is not surprising, given the overall cultural attitudes in which the system is being promoted. This is not a reflection upon the seikatsu writing movement, but is instead a common consideration about Japanese education and society as a whole. The fact that the seikatsu curriculum does not simply end with the first three steps, but postulates and projects steps four and five as being logical, culminating progressions, is a recognition of the world role into which Japan is growing. Japanese students need to be able to function also in the world where the "language of hypothesis" model is assumed.

If the existence of step four is the result of a need to build into the curriculum a level of abstraction that includes thesis building, then what makes step five a necessity? Step five is said to be not so much a step as a culmination; all of the learning that has been engendered in the first four steps should result in writer capabilities that can be characterized as step five. Does this mean, then, that step five contains nothing really unique? Our perception is that this step is characterized by one new factor: it formalizes the decisive shift in perspective from that of writer bias to that of reader bias. To be sure, this change in perspective develops steadily from the very beginning. Step five, however, acknowledges the accomplishment of the move to reader-biased writing. What matters by step five is much more the product than the process.

When we expressed our opinions at some seikatsu circle meetings about the writer-biased/reader-biased duality in which we could clarify our observations, teachers pointed out to us that reader awareness must be a factor as early as step two, with its explanatory function. Certainly that is so. And the way step four incorporates a thesis that must be accessible to a nonspecific readership is also evidence of strong movement toward the reader-biased end of the continuum. Still, it is not until step five that the following characterizations of writing are spelled out: the written product "should be communicative, persuasive, and/or moving" (Nihon Sakubun no Kai 1984:88). If we translate these qualities into Britton's three-part vision of language functions, these qualities are marks of either transactional or poetic writing.

In the objectives of the basic seikatsu curriculum, children are not overtly encouraged to manipulate the forms of language to embody their presentation as an artifact, except in writing poetry. To make such demands of them would divert their attention to the reader too soon. Instead, though, there is an exchange of social values that is paramount to the aims of seikatsu education. This exchange is played out by engaging the teacher as co-spectator with the child by means of both the student's self-expressive writing and the teacher's akapen response. In steps one through three this co-spectatorship relationship is fostered. The expansion of the audience to include classmates and the production of class anthologies (which implies a wider audience) promotes some branching toward either the transactional or the poetic end of the spectrum. The official transition, however, culminating in competence in transactional and poetic writing (the conspicuous shift toward the reader stance) is the reason, so it seems to us, that step five must be given a definitive place in the curriculum. Kokubun says of step five, "We have the vision culminating in the fifth step, but in fact it is not easy even for us teachers to produce writings of this nature, so we may just think of this as our faraway vision and wish" (1984b:95).

By projecting the curriculum through step five, there is a full acknowledgment of the language-arts responsibility of the seikatsu curriculum. Kokubun objectifies these responsibilities in the following goals: (1) to make sure that children know all the necessary components of the language-arts curriculum on writing; (2) to prepare them to meet the requirements for writing that will come up in job contexts, college, and so forth; (3) to prepare at least some of them to proceed into writing activities in various fields and capacities, including the writing of plays and fiction (1984b:94–95).

The problems the seikatsu movement has in realizing steps four and five, in light of the highly successful accomplishment of steps one through three, make an interesting contrast to traditional writing education here in America. In most writing programs here we have stressed what would correspond to steps four and five, without putting children through steps one, two, and three. Some of our students reach college-level proficiency in writing, but write empty prose. Often it is mechanically correct and glibly stated, but the English teacher complains that it glosses abstractly over the topic. If an international dialogue on writing were possible, it would be fascinating to see how some of the strengths of the seikatsu curriculum might be used as a foundation for our powerful secondary English courses, while the seikatsu movement itself could perhaps learn from those advanced rhetoric programs.

SEIKATSU CURRICULUM
IN LARGER EDUCATIONAL
CONTEXTS

CHAPTER **16** SEIKATSU CURRICULUM
IN LIGHT OF LANGUAGE-ARTS
EDUCATION IN THE WEST

In contrast to Japan's long history of early training in writer-biased prose, Western education has a rich experiential basis for formal, reader-directed writing education, culminating in college, if not before. In Japan, dedicated elementary-school teachers frequently lament the fact that test orientation in secondary schools has limited writing education to "non-prime time" coverage in many cases, which means that advanced writing training has not been fully developed. In America, high-school teachers ask how children can have gone through so many years of schooling without learning that they have something to write. Our educational systems differ for historical and cultural reasons.

Although excellent writing education programs are now beginning to flourish in some grade schools in America, the nation's pre-secondary-school teachers continue to resist calling themselves "English teachers." In Japan, on the other hand, the period of the day when reading, writing, grammar, punctuation, and other language skills are taught is a single period called "National Language" (namely, Japanese). Although some lessons feature one aspect of language more than another, there is not such an elaborate compartmentalization of skills and textbooks as usually occurs in American schools.

We have, until recently, been so preoccupied with reading education in America that an outsider might have assumed that we consider composition education in elementary school to be a frill. Fortunately, this is beginning to change. Many primary-grade teachers have elevated the status of writing to that of reading, but administrative guidelines still tend to indicate isolated skill development as the elementary school's basic responsibility in composition education. In a kind of reverse twist, the mechanical aspects of writing, such as handwriting, punctuation, and spelling, have been identified with the "Back to Basics" movement. Yet those are refinements of written language, not basics. They aid the reader who will see the text in the end, but offer little but distractions to the writer.

In the more extreme programs that give primacy to reader consid-erations, writing curricula utilize a series of learning packages to be mastered as a kind of initiation rite, prior to induction into the society of writers. To put the analogy another way, punctuation study, gram-

matical analysis, and paragraph formation are seen as stepping-stones
to get the student across the river to where the *real* English teacher
waits with the *real* secrets for those who succeed in making all the
right leaps. All too often, high-school teachers complain, by that time
the students have forgotten what it was they wanted to say.

Such reforms as the whole-language movement and the acceptance
of invented spelling have refocused attention in the West on what
children already know about language when they first come to school.
Under the philosophic umbrella of a whole-language focus, our beginning writers receive the same basics that Japanese children usually get,
namely, a chance to learn writing in a natural sequence of priorities,
just as they learned speech. It is a tenet of the whole-language approach
to teaching that "holistic instruction begins where it ends, with whole
language—mundane, useful, relevant, functional language—and moves
toward the full range of written language including literature in all its
variety" (Goodman and Goodman 1981:4). The seikatsu movement
shares the whole-language resource of beginning with "mundane, useful,
relevant, functional language" because the materials of the instruction
are children's actual compositions based upon real life. Skill mastery
is incorporated into writing as the need arises naturally.

Invented spelling simply allows children who are trying to express
themselves to make on-the-spot approximations of words they do not
know how to spell. Conventional spelling is valued, but not to the
point of interrupting an initial draft to achieve it. Japanese children are
doing invented spelling, even though it is not so described, when they
write in *hiragana* (see fn. 2, chapter 8). There is almost 100 percent
correspondence between the sounds of Japanese and the 46-some
syllabic symbols of *hiragana*. Furthermore, it is not considered a second-
class spelling system, since adults must regularly use it also as part of
the standard writing system.

Japanese is made up of a combination of ideographs and *hiragana*.
The ideographs are taught at an average rate of about 125 a year in
elementary school. Until an ideograph is learned, children write the
word in *hiragana*. This is one reason that first graders, once they have
mastered *hiragana*, can write so fluently in Japan. And, since mothers
and preschool teachers typically teach it before first grade, it is not
long into the beginning term before everyone can read and write with
that system. Still, when children feel confused as to which sound they
are hearing, seikatsu teachers encourage them to make a circle for the
symbol they cannot produce or determine and then go right on with
the writing. Also, if children speak a dialect, teachers understand that
they will begin by writing in that dialect as well.

When writers start with what they *can* do, namely, express something
in writing, rather than begin with what they *cannot* do, such as spell
in orthodox ways or punctuate to a reader's satisfaction, then we have
put the writer's needs first. This is the way that seikatsu education and
the acceptance of invented spelling both begin with the writer.

If we delay self-expressive writing because of the difficulties of English
spelling or the complexities of punctuation, it is because we have set
as a standard the final, edited texts of mature or professional writers.

affective filter

137

Seikatsu Curriculum
in Light of
Language-Arts
Education in the
West

Also, when we assume that a long, prior indoctrination period of reading literature will cause most children to internalize good models and make them good writers, we overlook the fact that they may become so skillful at reader analysis that they turn those same standards against their own initial attempts to write. Yet, if they write as they learn to read, the two skills naturally develop in tandem, nurturing each other. Children in Japan read good literature, both in their National Language textbooks and from trade books, but they also study compositions written by children of their own age, so they internalize standards for writing that grow up as they do.

In the interplay of research and teaching that occurred when Graves engaged in a lengthy research project in a New Hampshire school (see Graves 1983), it was discovered that children progress more confidently when professionally published writing is treated in the same fashion as children's own compositions. When fledgling authors in the classroom hear their writing discussed in depth with the same intensity as a favorite trade book, there is enough carryover in their future writing that it does not matter if that sort of intensive feedback only occurs at widely spaced intervals. In this aspect, the Graves model and seikatsu teachers' experiences coincide. With so many children per class in Japan, some children wait a long time between sessions in which their compositions are singled out for appreciation by the whole class. But the intensity of the experience of having one's writing used for as much as a 45-minute lesson makes for lasting benefits. And the akapen response supports the child individually in the meantime.

In terms of revision, it is a philosophical decision in seikatsu tradition to concentrate upon the heuristic moments of writing rather than the explication of insight for a reader. Most teachers do expect children to proofread and edit. Sometimes additional information is inserted as well. But major overhauling and a series of prefinal drafts are not commonly expected. Kokubun admonishes teachers to remember the natural development of children and says:

> Up through about the fourth grade, we should not criticize children for lack of organization. . . . Children are not writing a piece of literature. What is most important is to plunge into writing . . . without inhibition . . . as though the threads of letters come pouring out from the tip of their pencils. It is here that we see the healthy state of children's writing. (Kokubun 1952:56).

Graves also describes revision as "not necessarily a natural act. It draws upon a different source of energy, the energy of *anticipation*" (Graves 1983:160). Although anticipation is a factor in almost any writing, it involves a reader-awareness level that seikatsu proponents would rather contain within bounds so as to leave the writer-self fairly unencumbered. Graves looks for the breakthroughs in writing education in the interplay between the "forward vision" (the vision of the imprint of information on classmates or in publication) and "backward vision" (toward the event or original conception) (1983:160). Seikatsu philosophy tends to downplay the anticipation of audience reaction for beginning writers in favor of stronger writer-experience connections. Although children soon begin to anticipate the teacher's akapen response and the possibility of having their writing discussed in class, these audience reactions are usually focused upon the writer, the reported experience, and the interplay between those factors, rather than on communicative skill or the impact of the writing upon the reader.

Hiroko Iwatani explained to us the reluctance to insist upon revision:

We want to value the moment of inspiration when the child writes the first draft, so we cannot ask for major revision; there is a crescendo that occurs, and to expect the child to completely reorganize his writing would be to lessen that effect.

The seikatsu teacher puts selfhood and self-expression, the immediate goals of this kind of writing education, in a position of primacy. The complex process of learning to project oneself to the "other side of the text" is seen as a potential threat to the self-awareness and reality-connectedness of beginning writers. Teachers in English-speaking countries are being encouraged by researchers to look more tolerantly on expressive writing and to avoid rushing to reader-biased preoccupations. Teachers who adhere to seikatsu practices in Japan do so in the belief that the self-expressive aspects of writing enhance the child's perception of the world. This seems to be a potential meeting point between the two educational systems. Behind this point of convergence, however, there is the division of tradition that puts the West's system in a reader-biased category that contrasts sharply with Japan's.

The writer bias we noted in seikatsu practice was somewhat evident even in the non-seikatsu classes we observed. In reading lessons as well as in class discussion of student writing, the teachers' questioning usually led to the searching out of the writer's perspective. In Japanese classes there is a subtle, but cumulatively noticeable, persistence in using textual evidence to try to pin down the writer's insights and intentions. In contrast, questions in American English classes seem designed to evaluate the success or failure of the writing in terms of the reader, as a piece of communication.

A seikatsu teacher made a transcript of a recorded post-writing appreciation session (Inoue 1983:52–55). Once he had launched his fourth graders into a discussion by eliciting a few general reactions, he guided the rest of the session by three basic questions. These three questions are listed below, but we omitted the children's responses and the teacher's further elicitations on the same questions to emphasize the three basic strands of the discussion:

What could it have been that made Shishido-kun [the author] want to write? . . .

Now that you have been thinking about what Shishido-kun wanted to write, how was he able to express what he wanted to say? . . .

What experiences have you had like those Shishido-kun wrote about? . . .

139

Seikatsu Curriculum
in Light of
Language-Arts
Education in the
West

The first two-thirds or so of the discussion dealt with Shishido's intention to write and his experience in making the writing express what he intended. That is a shift in emphasis from reader-oriented discussion of a text. Of course, this was a classmate's paper, not a piece of literature, but we noticed that the same sorts of questions were often asked in reading classes as well.

Instead of this writer bias, questions such as the following would have been indicative of a reader emphasis:

"What occurred to you as you read about Shishido's efforts?"

"Is there more a reader needs to know about this experience?"

"Would someone from another class or school understand this composition?"

"What effect was gained by the description of the many failures to do the stunt?"

"How did the story hold your interest through to the end?"

Such questions typify the sorts of things teachers in the West tend to ask in dealing with literature as well as when leading a group in critiquing a student's writing. They reflect our traditional reader-biased concerns and are an effort to link the text more closely with the reader, which is also the task of a reader-conscious writer. If authors listen in on such a session about their own text, presumably they will be better able to meet audience expectations in the future.

In reader-oriented education, we assume that we can test readers' competence by measuring their interaction with the text and we can test writers' competence by measuring the bond that unites reader and text. If the writer communicated effectively, that bond should be powerful in some way. In writer-oriented education, if the objective of writing is to solidify the self in relation to some reality, then good readers may vicariously gain from an understanding of the writer's perspective, but the primary concern is for writers to intensify their bond with the content of the self-discovery process.

In this vein, Shishido's classmates were directed to consider his intentions as a writer and his fulfillment of those intentions. Then they moved to the question that teachers here also use to open up a topic: "What experiences have you had like those?"

Shishido had described his struggle to learn the gymnastics stunt on a horizontal bar that we call in English "skinning the cat." The excerpt below presents some of his efforts:

FINALLY I LEARNED TO "SKIN THE CAT"

. . . Watanabe-kun came. He can skin the cat eighty-eight times. He's an expert. I said to Watanabe-kun, "Teach me." Watanabe-kun, looking over my way, said, "Yeah." Looking at me in the face, Watanabe said, "Okay, Shishido, try it now." I said, "Yeah" and looked at the bar. I hooked my leg over it and shouted inside myself, "Ready, Set, Now." I felt my hands shaking from the strain. About halfway up, my leg slipped off and I tried to force it back, hitting the bar so hard I screamed, "Ow." And I dropped down like falling from the bar. I looked at my leg and it was blue.

I began to lose interest in practice, but I wanted to get as close as possible to CAN-DO. *First I hooked my leg on and tried to go around, but I failed. And I tried again and failed again. . . .*

Matsuda-kun said in a loud voice, "Shishidooo, youuu, your leg slips off so easily. How about if you put the tip of your right foot to brace your left leg?" . . . I looked around and Watanabe was skinning the cat. He lifts himself up and, with a big motion, goes swoop and circles the bar. Then Watanabe taught me how to lift myself up that way. . . . Finally I was about 3/4 ready to give up, but I tried again. Swoop. I made it a little more than halfway and Matsuda-kun pushed me so I could make it. So I tried once more with 4/4, that is to say one-whole, confidence. "I made it!" I said loudly. I was not so happy that I almost jumped up, I really did jump up. Everyone was happy for me, so that made me even happier.

Then, there was the end-of-term ceremony so we lined up. I was hot. The northwind was blowing gently on me. . . .[1]

His classmates had considered how the struggle to learn to do a new trick had been the impetus for writing, and they had evaluated the writing against Shishido's presumed intentions. From there, the students' attention moved beyond the writing, to a study of life itself. The text had served its purpose; Shishido's basic theme, persistence in overcoming failure, and his specific vehicle, gymnastic stunts, became the agenda for discussion.

The typical seikatsu teacher leads a discussion that focuses first upon the connection making of the writer and then upon the experience, or reality, illustrated by that writing. This enables teachers to juggle writing-proficiency goals with self-development aims during the same lessons. As noted by William K. Cummings, Japanese elementary-school teachers are strong advocates of whole-person education, choosing for themselves such goals as "to develop children with pure and rich hearts" and "to encourage the will to endure in whatever is attempted" (1980:13). Seikatsu teachers epitomize these whole-person educators, both historically and in present practice, because they constantly measure the national curriculum against the reality of their students' lives. Western educators who also struggle to make education authentic and relevant share a bond with the seikatsu teachers in this effort.

CHAPTER **SEIKATSU WRITING IN AN AMERICAN CONTEXT**

In 1984–85, after our stay in Japan, I returned to a fourth- and fifth-grade class in a neighborhood nicknamed Old Pascua Village, even though this "village" is now engulfed by Tucson near the old downtown section. The languages of Old Pascua Village are Spanish, English, and Yaqui. The children seem to have a strong cultural tendency for cooperation and noncompetitive learning. By the same token, many seem to consider that putting themselves forward in class would be antisocial behavior. Coincidentally, these traits are in accord with the egalitarian Japanese elementary-school climate, where it is group, not individual, accomplishments that earn the highest praise.

It was not my intention to transplant the seikatsu system, but rather to find out what application and merit it would have for my students. So I launched them into journal writing with seikatsu stress on "one strong memory, one that you really want to express." Rather than letting them log in the entire day, I asked them to look for one aspect of the past day or so that stood out in their memories for any reason. I asked them to write it with as many details as possible. Then, I tried to emulate the seikatsu teachers by reading into the writing whatever intentions I could detect. It was a pleasant task, and the journals soon began to take on individual characteristics. One child typically asked some form of the question "Did anything like that ever happen to you, Teacher?" I shared more of my childhood with her than I ever had with any other student. Another sometimes used the journal to campaign indirectly for things like more P. E. One girl not only wrote copiously, but also went back through her journal periodically, rereading and answering my akapen comments. I would see her going back through old journal entries making additions, then it would be my turn to answer all of those. Often this went back and forth until the pages filled with real dialogues. We had our own private women's-liberation discussions in a humorous vein.

In trying to learn to insert effective akapen responses, I tried to imagine myself as a spontaneously responding reader looking right over the child's shoulder at the time of writing: "Oh, no. Imagine Tony

Note: In this chapter, we use "I" to refer to Mary.

141

trying to hide quietly and then having to sneeze!'' or ''You have included *every* detail of how you cooked that egg. I can almost smell it.''

My relationship with some students differed in these exchanges from the way we interacted in person, so these akapen comments of mine were more than just an extension of what I would say if I could conference with every child on every bit of writing all of the time. As I began to get over a sense of artificiality, I realized that the student and I were creating a ''history'' with each other that did not exist on any other level of our relationship. It seemed to bolster the public relationship we had in class. Furthermore, unlike the missed opportunities that occur *every* day in class, I could dwell upon my response at length in answering a journal. I did not, however, solve the problem of how coercive to be about requiring journal writing, so some students wrote as little as they could, turning in an empty journal except when I required them to write.

Students' journal entries were the models for writing longer personal narratives all during the fall. Surprisingly, no one asked to write fiction. I was so unnerved by the absence of student complaints on this point that I could not resist testing their complacency. In November I tentatively offered that it would be all right if they wanted to use make-believe for their next piece of writing (a clear departure from seikatsu practice). Two children wrote fantasies based upon chess pieces, in accord with their newly acquired love of the game, but most students deviated only slightly from the personal-experience mode, merely stretching the truth for a climactic ending. One such example was Debbie's story of a cousin who really does love Mickey Mouse and so has a birthday party with a Mickey Mouse theme; all was plausible until the Mickey Mouse–shaped birthday cake came to life for an attempted getaway. Her writing was quite successful.

It does seem that children's imaginations are a resource in writing that I do not want to deny them, particularly in our American context. On the other hand, if left completely to their imaginative devices, many children seem to have great difficulty maintaining the thread of fiction or fantasy. They exert so much effort choosing from the infinite possibilities that they tend to run out of enthusiasm or get twisted into a hopeless web of complexities. A strong rooting in personal narrative does seem to be an easier base on which to learn to write. I look forward to the consideration of genre as a topic of research and discussion that will enable teachers to help students more.

As a foray into step two writing, I asked the students to interview a family member or friend with an interesting job or hobby. A few of them wrote the interviews entirely as narrative accounts, but most automatically switched, at the beginning or after a narrative introduction, into step two form (explanation and generalization). Without any teaching of step two directly, the few model compositions and the students' natural use of language for that situation made such writing easy. Their personal narrative practice gave some, such as Virginia, a natural way to begin:

I wanted to know more about art, and I have an uncle that is an artist. I asked him if I could interview him about art. He agreed. And we were going to begin Mon. Nov. 26, 1984 at 6:30 P.M.

It was Mon. 6:30 P.M. I asked my uncle Ramon if he was ready for the interview. He said, "I guess. Let's go to the kitchen." . . .

Virginia's shy and sensitive humor comes through to me when I read into this introduction the way she pinned her uncle down in getting to give her the prearranged interview. Like many of my students, she is more likely to understate than overdramatize a scene. This piece rings with Virginia-authenticity.

During all of the first semester I needlessly worried that students might get bored with doing the same sorts of writing, so I was puzzled when students seemed satisfied to write in just two genres: personal narratives and descriptive writing. Finally I realized that they were probably enjoying the comfort of familiarity by having opportunities to write extensively in the same modes. Instead of having to adjust to different expectations from me, the variety they were exploring was in the topics that writer-biased prose opens up. When their compositions were appreciated in class, we used the seikatsu attitudes of seeking out the writer's intentions and expressing respect and admiration when those intentions were realized, rather than voicing our own concern for enlightenment or entertainment.

In February, we took a break from prose to explore poetry. I merely encouraged free verse and helped students decide upon the form by empowering their own instincts. In other words, my questions in response to the poems they showed me were usually couched in terms of "How do you like the way it sounds?" or "Does it carry out what you wanted it to be?" It was seikatsu poetry in the sense that I encouraged them to think of a poem as a single picture or image, and to choose words that fit that picture. Seikatsu teachers talk about a single heart surge. I did not know how to express that to my students, but Erlinda produced such a poem on her own:

ROSE
Oh, rose, why did you stick me?
Does it hurt to be picked?
If it does, I won't do it.
But I'll still visit you,
And bring you water.

The students expressed a desire to write again based upon primary research, but I was reluctant to send them out for more interviews. Another step two writing task that seemed to give them some of the same involvement and was in accord with the seikatsu assignment pattern was the introduction of a person. I asked them to write a profile of someone well known to them.

I myself wanted to experiment with a longer prewriting stage, to see if extending the rehearsal process, as in the seikatsu curriculum, would have a positive effect upon their fluency and organization. Working all together and in pairs for several days, they read compositions translated from Japanese and discussed possible topics with a partner. My major modification of the seikatsu pattern was this encouragement of peer interchanges all through the writing process. Listening partners became writing partners, available for collaboration, for those who felt comfortable doing so. Besides consulting their partner during the writing, children who felt ready for a final draft could check first with editors, one each for organization, punctuation, spelling, and paragraphing.

Another variation, which we never observed in Japan, but which is strongly advocated by the Bay Area Writing Project and its affiliates in this country, was that all adults in the room participated as writers. I wrote about my mother-in-law, sharing my decision processes and drafts in class, and a visitor who observed the class for two weeks also went through the entire writing process by acting as a listening/writing partner and by writing about her grandfather.

I introduced planning sheets, based upon those we saw Hino's students use in Japan (see chapter 12). Not all students actually used these forms, but the effect of spending a few periods with them was to lengthen the time between conceiving of a topic and actually writing it. Interesting things occurred during the interval between deciding on the topic and beginning to write. Normally students would already be writing during the time it took Debbie, for example, to try out at least seven titles such as "My Cousin Vicky," "Vicky My Best Friend," "Vicky as a Sister." She wrote them all on a piece of scratch paper and spent about fifteen minutes considering and crossing out titles until she ended up with "Me and Vicky." This proved to be more than a title search, for, when she later wrote her lead sentence, it was "To me Vicky is like a sister or a best friend, but she is really my cousin," and she followed that lead with three paragraphs of specific examples about their special relationship. Like the children whose struggle for just the right topic resulted in writing that seemed embedded in their own control, Debbie's efforts for the right beginning set up for her a cohesive framework for writing.

Armando's titles also went through many metamorphoses. His older sister is given extra responsibilities at home while their parents launch a fledgling restaurant business. When Armando worked on his planning sheet, he started with the title "Silvia is a Mother?" Over the next few days he experimented with "Silvia, a Mother to Me," "Sister or Mother?" "The Real Truth About Silvia" (jokingly), and others. The final writing was titled "How Silvia Lives."

Armando's subtitles included Cooking, Cleaning Up, Radio, Mean and Nice, Bossy, The Beginning, Outside, The Phone, and Working. Many of the notes under these contained some of the flippancy to be expected, perhaps, when a ten-year-old writes about his fourteen-year-old sister. Study of his rough draft and final copy, however, shows how the image of Silvia evolved into a fairly objective rendering, with Armando's presence largely limited to the voice of the author. This is part of the final version:

HOW SILVIA LIVES

My sister Silvia is about 14 years old. Silvia's birthday is on December 15.

Silvia is always cleaning the house. She gives everyone chores, so you might think she has the least chores, but she has the most chores. She has to clean the kitchen, the living room and both bathrooms, including vacuuming, mopping, washing dishes and both toilets.

Silvia is usually watching videos on television or listening to the radio, all while she is cleaning the house. She listens to the radio so long and watches videos on TV so long that she knows a lot of songs by heart.

Silvia is always cooking us dinner. She thinks that she is the worst cook; sometimes I think so too. But when she makes something I hate to eat, she makes it really good. Silvia's cooking is the third best in the family, next to my mom's and dad's. . . .

A commonality between the seikatsu philosophy and the process approach is the idea that a topic is not necessarily milked dry by one composition about it. Calkins also refers to topics as sources that can be mined over and over (lecture, February 8, 1985). In this composition Armando was recycling an old topic with a new variation: earlier he had written in his journal about the time when his parents gathered all of the children into the living room and explained how both of them had quit their jobs in order to venture into the restaurant business for themselves; he had written a composition describing the way chores are divided among the children in his family; and he had composed a poem about work. Even his journal entry in early fall, detailing his first solo cooking experience, reflects his role in his parents' new occupational demands. Armando's struggle to decide upon the best title for his piece about his sister signifies the importance of this topic to him, but he worked through some of his own involvement with Silvia in the writer-biased earlier version. His earliest draft described some of the conflicts of having a sister in a semi-mothering role, but the final version is a portrait of his sister from a more self-removed perspective. Armando has excellent control of writing in many dimensions. He can write to sort out his own perspectives, and he can write to inform or impress a reader. He has access to writing for both writer-biased and reader-biased purposes.

A frequently raised question about personal narratives, and a question about which I share concern, is whether or not writing about themselves encourages children to spill more of their personal lives onto paper than is appropriate. I caution my students that "secrets written may not remain secret." This applies to personal, family, cultural, and religious secrets, for most of my students belong to an ethnic group which has rituals not to be shared with outsiders. In case they do write in a personal way, I respect their ownership of the text by giving them the option of sharing it only with me. Most seikatsu teachers have devised some way to handle the same problem. Writer-biased writing, by definition, is not necessarily for public consumption.

Carmen had written a poem in February about her grandmother's funeral. In selecting a subject to profile in March she seemed both drawn and resistant to the idea of writing again about her grandmother. She was very restless in talking through this topic with her partner, saying often that she was going to think of someone else. In the end she wrote a highly expressive description of her relationship with her grandmother, about memories from before and during her final illness. I use the word "expressive" for her composition in the sense of its being extremely writer-biased prose. It was writing "close to the self" and contained many speechlike phrases. Sections such as "The last thing I remember was I was watching somebody get out of the elevator. I think I slept at the hospital because my grandmother had to stay there" and "After three weeks or more, because I don't remember, she died" seemed to be Carmen's sincere effort to sort out the details for herself as much as for a reader. Carmen is a very capable writer. Her reader-biased writing would not show this wavering over details. She seemed to have been sorting out what she remembered without categorizing details according to reader interest, without trying to present a clean, clear view that a reader could appreciate. When she indicated that she did not really want to write on this topic, she may have meant that she did not feel ready to do the polished, reader-biased style of which she is also capable. Yet she seemed drawn to work on the sorting-out process. Her composition ended, "I still have some memories of her. That's why I am writing about her."

Sometimes it takes longer for a writer-biased author to work through the inner decisions and achieve a composition that can be appreciated by a general audience, but there is no real shortcut to writing that serves the writer as well as the reader. Only when authors control the whole process, including sometimes agonizing over what they want to express, does the writing belong uniquely to the writer. Rushing through to reader-biased prose may bypass this function of writing.

The variations between writer concern and reader emphasis reveal themselves in the myriad of daily decisions that teachers make. As a case in point, I have rethought the following experience I had several years ago, before I knew much about either the seikatsu philosophy or the process approach to teaching writing.

A fourth-grade boy named Joaquin wrote a personal narrative that began in the following way: "It was the funeral of A—— and I was dancing with Paul. I was sad because A—— had died . . ." The text went on to describe primarily Joaquin's emotions at that time, including wanting some ice cream that he could not have. It was writing that had many gaps in information, which would puzzle a reader who did not know the context. The student is a Yaqui Indian, a member of a tribe now recognized as American Indians. The Yaquis, who came from Mexico within the last hundred years, brought with them an indigenous form of Catholicism that includes ritual dancing by members of various functional societies within each community. This boy's classmates and I knew that he and Paul were both members of a society that has the responsibility for performing certain dances at funerals.

Until Joaquin's text reaches a generalized audience, the writing is a powerful testimony to his selfhood. It does nothing, however, for the uninformed reader's comprehension about Yaqui Indian ceremonies and may actually mislead such a reader. If I had been a seikatsu-oriented teacher at that time, I would probably have had him share the writing in the classroom with a positive response.

As it was, I thought of the same composition in the hands of a teacher at the junior high school across town, where Joaquin would be sent three years later. I pushed him to look at this writing from afar, as a general audience would see it. It took three conferences, which fact alone should have caused me to reconsider my timing. This student was not yet ready to internalize the perspectives of people who are not part of his closely knit community. He had trouble imagining any reader who needed to be told what seemed so obvious to him. I regret to admit that I finally told Joaquin to think of a lady from New York City, on a first visit to Tucson, with no knowledge of Yaqui culture. If she somehow got hold of this writing, I told him, she would be surprised, because she would think that he and Paul were dancing as people dance at the local dance hall, and she would wonder what all that dancing had to do with a funeral. Suddenly, with an expression that showed both enlightenment and dismay, Joaquin snatched back the paper and poised his pencil over the first sentence. Then he stopped. "But what can I do?" he said.

Everything that I know now about that writing and the writer as he was then tells me that he wrote writer-biased prose, and as such, it was not inadequate writing. He had made a firm connection with reality and had a strong motivation to express that connection in writing. For the readership in our classroom he even had audience awareness. Ironically, once he becomes aware of generalized-reader needs, he might struggle hard, only to come up with the very same two opening sentences as a way of capturing the reader's attention: "It was the funeral of A—— and I was dancing with Paul. I was sad because A—— had died."

Learning to write is a developmental process. My insertion of the clarifying sentences I could add to Joaquin's product would not have enhanced the learning process. It is over a long series of writings that the student takes control of the interplay between writer and reader; I was trying to impose this upon Joaquin prematurely.

In the writing unit described earlier in this chapter, many students wrote profiles that referred to ethnic activities that an outsider would not understand. My seikatsu writing philosophy exposure now leads me to tread softly rather than hasten them toward writing for a general audience. Yet something in me still produces a sense of urgency to be sure that these students will someday attain communicative competence for a general readership. How I welcomed, therefore, the peer interaction between Virginia and Armando, who was serving as her punctuation editor. He persisted in questioning a paragraph that would have been clear had he known more about the Easter ceremonies of the Yaqui tribe. She finally explained it to his satisfaction, but he could not find a way to resolve his difficulty with a punctuation change, so he yielded to her on the basis of her oral clarification. Then, when he went back to his own work, Virginia sat and stared at the offending paragraph. The next day, when I praised her specificity in the first three paragraphs, Virginia asked me what I thought of the problem section of the fourth paragraph. I agreed that it could be misread and we worked together to expand that part with the needed qualifying statement.

I think that collaborative practices in the classroom are my way of assuaging reader-biased demands. By biting my own tongue, I can maintain myself in the role of a reader with a writer bias, and by encouraging collaboration, the students may pace themselves toward a sense of audience. The extensive use of class discussions in seikatsu lesson planning seems to be a way of solving the same dilemma, that is, how to move toward reader awareness within a strongly writer-oriented framework. From our observations, it seems that many variations of this solution exist in Japanese seikatsu classrooms as well.

CHAPTER **IX**

**JAPANESE EDUCATION AND
SEIKATSU TSUZURIKATA**

"K-chan is an *ichinensei* [first grader]!"

"A-san is studying for his college entrance exams!"

Between these two statements there is a world of difference. K-chan, our composite picture of the Japanese school entrant, is the object of greater national attention than her American counterpart. For months before the early April entrance ceremony (the school year is April to March in Japan, with a summer vacation from late July through August) the media have capitalized on the emotional high of this event. Any child who has become six by the beginning of April may begin first grade. K-chan is likely to have had from one to three years of pre-schooling, privately funded, but it is the first-grader image that sells everything from noodles to life insurance. Stores blare repetitious reminders to grandparents and other relatives to assure that they have purchased the symbolic and functional, but expensive, leather backpack for her. The image of the first grader is that of a bright-eyed, resolute child marching proudly into the world of study.

The image of the Japanese high-school senior, however, is that of a red-eyed, battle-weary teenager who resolutely studies into the wee hours of the morning and has foresworn all other activities but cramming. Television commercials use his image to sell vitamins and energy-lifting fast foods. Some of the Walkman headsets plugged into adolescent ears on the trains in Japan are pumping in English vocabulary instead of rock music. A-san's parents may well have restructured their own social lives around his study schedule and the financial burden of special tutelage. A windup model of A-san can be purchased in any novelty shop; it is a toy student cramming so hard that the pupils in his bleary eyes are whirling spirals while he frantically jots down words in a notebook.

Japan has one of the most open educational systems in the world. Not class or birth, but educational achievement paves the way to success. Of course some of this achievement can be purchased in the private-study marketplace, but a few critical tests on a few critical days allow anyone to aim for elite status.

Compulsory education, the first through the ninth grades, is extremely egalitarian (see Cummings 1980). Furthermore, it is well supported as public education. In 1981 over 99 percent of elementary-school children and more than 95 percent of junior high schoolers were enrolled in public schools, according to the Ministry of Education's 1982 report. These schools scrupulously keep themselves and their classrooms as heterogeneous as their attendance areas allow. Children are not dubbed sparrows or nightingales according to reading prowess, for ability grouping is considered to be demoralizing and undemocratic during the compulsory education years.

Even though high school, tenth grade through twelfth, is not compulsory, about 94 percent of the appropriate age group go on to this level (NHK news report, July 8, 1984). However, severe stratification takes place at the point of high-school entrance. Each high school uses examinations to eliminate students competitively. Some also take into consideration junior-high grades, recommendations, and aptitude tests. Students select their high school from those open to them after this screening, often commuting for an hour or more to get to school each day.

Until such stratification looms, however, K-chan and her classmates are expected to share in the responsibility for one another's learning. One of the observations made by Cummings (1980:130–31) that our class visits confirm is that a student's weak performance in elementary school tends to be covered up in class. Teachers behave as if every student is capable. Lessons are structured so that the better students indirectly compensate for the poorer students' inabilities. For example, nearly everything is read aloud, even in the upper grades. This may partly be explained as a way to be sure that the *kanji* characters, or ideographs, which usually have many possible readings, are learned with the correct pronunciation for that context; but it also enables unskillful readers to follow along and participate in subsequent discussions. Key points are usually written on the board, and some students in the classes we observed seemed to be more involved in copying these notes than in contributing to the interchange of ideas. Seatmates frequently help each other. Often students are directed to move their desks from the usual double rows into groups and to consult each other for a consensus before contributing the group's answer to the class. It is true that one student often is given or takes leadership, but there seemed to be a substantially wide range of participation in the group work we observed. We felt that this reflects a strong background in interpersonal responsibility. Although there were students who seemed to be marking time, there were few who appeared to be totally lost, in spite of the lockstep progression and lack of individualization in the curriculum.

From junior high school on, memorization of *kanji* characters maintains an important role in education. In the elementary grades there are presently 996 characters that students are required to learn to read, according to the 1983 national curriculum guide; they are also expected to learn to write most of these. By the end of the ninth grade, however, the student must have mastered nearly double that number. A great deal of homework, then, is dictionary/vocabulary study. The junior high school classes we observed began with a brief *kanji* quiz.

Even those high schools that weigh middle-school grades in their entrance decisions tend to put more emphasis on academic subjects than on such things as fine arts. So, although K-chan's teachers might actively design lessons to make her a "whole person," including the use of seikatsu writing experiences, A-san's teachers may only hope for the same accomplishment through whatever club activities, sports, and interpersonal relationships the study schedule allows. Also, there may be greater emphasis in Japan upon the discipline of *persisting* than there is in American schools. Whereas in the United States, students utilize time in secondary schools to explore many interests and a wide range of possible talents, both as career planning and for personal development, Japanese students are encouraged to select only one extracurricular activity and devote themselves to greater mastery of it. Even at that, A-san will probably drop out of his club during his final year of high school. Even one extracurricular activity at that time may be more than his schedule allows.

In terms of seikatsu writing education, K-chan's odds of finding herself under the guidance of a proponent of this method diminish sharply when she leaves elementary school and even more when she enters high school. This is unfortunate, as one extremely successful high-school teacher, Eiko Kouda, told us, because it is precisely during the infamous "examination hell" that students need a counterweight such as seikatsu writing: "it can open a critical window into the real world of their lives that they might otherwise ignore, and it enables them to talk to each other—get into each other's heads—at a time in their lives when they would otherwise be too busy for anything but superficial chatter."

How do K-chan and her uninhibited classmates become A-san and his study-strained cohorts? From the first day, when some of K-chan's friends are boisterously vying for the teacher's attention, to the last year, when many of A-san's friends are too intent on absorbing information to volunteer their opinions, what occurs in the years that intervene? We studied in depth only certain aspects of the language-arts curriculum and that largely in the first six grades, but the most succinct way to explain what we saw is an increasing funneling of students toward examinations, with a gradual exclusion of diversionary, self-exploratory opportunities.

The school we visited to establish for ourselves a basis for "typical" elementary-school education is in a Tokyo suburb. K-chan came with her mother to the opening ceremony for first graders; she was dressed in a new dress, and her mother in a lovely kimono. Her daddy stayed long enough to take their picture and then rushed off to commute (late) to work in Tokyo. The little boys had on new suits. Some mothers wore Western dresses, but everyone was formally attired. In the auditorium, amidst flowers and banners, the school band played and the chorus sang. Telegrams of congratulations from local kindergartens and the school board were read. A second grader read his welcoming speech, and there were special speeches by the principal, vice-principal, and PTA president. The principal seemed most concerned with instructing the children in home etiquette related to leaving home in the morning and returning in the afternoon. He built upon their status as first graders. No mention was made of study or homework; rather, the new opportunities for friendship were described.

Japanese parents are known to be easy on their young children, but they too take advantage of the mystique surrounding entrance into first grade. We saw one parent discipline her son on a bus one evening by scolding him, "You're a first grader now, so you should know better than to jump all over the seats."

Home visits are part of every teacher's responsibility, and authority over the children is shared between home and school. If K-chan's fourth-grade brother develops a passion for video games that his teacher considers excessive, she might consider it part of her responsibility to visit the home to make suggestions about parental guidance. At the same time, if a student gets caught shoplifting in the local department store, the parents may question the teacher's moral guidance. Adults usually attempt to present a united front to the younger generation. When differences do exist, they are sometimes complicated by the overlapping domains of home and school.

Uniforms are not common in public elementary school but are usual from middle school through high school. Dress codes vary according to locale and school, but some are so strict that students of either sex with naturally curly hair must verify by certificate that their hair has not been curled by a permanent.

Although such stringency may loom in K-chan's future, her transition from home to school as a first grader is purposely made very gradual. First and second graders stay for the full six-period day only twice a week. Teachers ease them into routines and generally ignore their misconduct. Just as mothers in Japan often avoid confrontations with small children who behave willfully, teachers manipulate children's natural peer pressure to subtly achieve cooperation rather than mere submission to authority. Attention is lavished upon those who respond positively. The teachers we watched rewarded the students' contributions with their full attention, even when other children were being disruptive or inattentive. They rarely resorted to any indication of disapproval. They seemed to rely on rapidly moving the lesson along as a primary way of holding the attention of the majority at the expense of the ones who could not, or would not, participate. The only exception was a quick look and murmur of a child's name when bad behavior seemed to be on the verge of becoming contagious.

Before first-grade lessons begin in earnest, the teacher seeks to establish group interdependence as well as personal self-assurance. Students learn to share the daily janitorial chores, cleaning bathrooms, halls, offices, and school grounds. They function as teams responsible to each other for successful completion of assignments. It is economical for schoolchildren to take over daily school maintenance work, but the primary objective is to establish responsibility and cooperation. At the end of the school year everyone from the principal on down pitches in to give the school a complete spring cleaning. Students also take turns serving lunch to their classmates, again operating as a team. Class

A. *Lunch is delivered to each classroom, where it is served by a team of students.*

B. *When everyone has been served, the leaders signal that children may begin eating.*

mottoes and group rewards, such as certificates from the principal, intensify the spirit of group accomplishment.

While such an orientation is being solidified, the first-grade teacher uses the early weeks to ascertain which children need help to catch up with the rest in such skills as reading and writing the *hiragana* (phonetic) alphabet, which many have learned at home or in preschool. Since the group is expected to move ahead at one pace, this lining up at the starting line is considered critical. Once launched, faster students are used as models and peer tutors to keep others moving, but the teacher never makes elaborate allowances for individualization. Faster children are allowed to "perform" more often, both for the sake of modeling and just to maintain their interest, but otherwise they are expected to move ahead with the group, just as slower children must try to do.

The full school day is usually six forty-five-minute periods, broken by five- or ten-minute breaks, a long lunch break, and a clean-up period. There may be class meeting time or club meetings at either end of the day. Saturday classes last only until noon, and Sunday is a day off (or extra time for cram school, however one wants to look at it).

Classmates often stay together for two grades, frequently with the same teacher. Although class groupings are reshuffled periodically to assure heterogeneity, K-chan is nearly certain to progress to the end of ninth grade at the same pace as her classmates because retentions are almost unknown. Even in secondary school, promotion is almost automatic if the student attends fairly often and behaves acceptably. The juggling skill of the teacher becomes the knack of moving the class along fast enough to meet the national standards while picking up and dragging along any stragglers so that the pace can be maintained.

The number of hours prescribed by the Ministry of Education for "National Language" (all aspects of Japanese language arts including reading, composition, spelling, grammar, and handwriting) varies slightly according to grade level. In general, the number of language-arts instructional periods (about forty-five minutes each) a year averages about one a day, with slightly less in grades five and six. Within the National Language curriculum, composition education is mandated to be three-tenths of the program. (Considering the complexity of the Japanese language, it may seem like a small part of the curriculum to make reading as little as seven-sixtieths of the total curriculum in elementary school, but formal training in reading Japanese extends further into secondary school than reading education per se in America.)

Near the end of first grade, we watched K-chan and her classmates finish a series of reading lessons from their National Language book on a Japanese translation of "Frog Gets a Letter" by Arnold Lobel. K-chan's teacher is not a seikatsu proponent. The same textbook interspersed writing lessons with reading selections, and each task in writing was to achieve a product in the style of the previous reading selection. Since Frog had received a letter in the story, the children moved from that series of lessons into a unit on letter writing. In accordance with the curriculum and the textbook, students' writing lessons were organized around various functions of written expression. Later lessons would teach the writing of "how-to" instructions, reports, stories (real and fictional), and so forth. In addition to learning a format, students study appropriate mechanical skills, such as punctuation.

Seikatsu education, as we have said, is process, not product, driven. Its aim is inner growth through writing rather than skill mastery or form learning. Personal narrative writing, which makes up but a minor part of the writing for K-chan in this school, is the norm during most of elementary school for children in a seikatsu classroom. On the other hand, seikatsu teachers are in no way excused from following the national curriculum. Therefore, they must balance its requirements with their own goals, assuring those in administrative control that the children in their classes are not being deprived of full access to all the knowledge and skills prescribed. How this is carried out in actuality varies from teacher to teacher. But having children write journals at home and share their writing during the class meeting time at either end of the day often provides extra time during the regular school sessions.

We did not receive a uniform answer as to how seikatsu teachers handle the writing of fiction when the textbook calls for it (fiction, as noted throughout this book, is downplayed greatly in the seikatsu plan). What may have to suffice for an answer is what one teacher told us: "At least, when we do teach these things we do not call it seikatsu tsuzurikata."

K-chan may not have any seikatsu teachers if the present staff remains intact during her six years at this school. She will have some excellent training in form and style and will probably write more realism than fantasy. Except for the possibility that she will not have to fill in so many workbooks, there will not be much in her language-arts training that differs from what is typical in American classrooms that adhere to textbooks. If she has the teacher we saw in third grade, she might be expected to keep a journal. However, instead of elaborate dialogue with an akapen, the teacher's response will more typically be a single, general comment and a flower symbol that is the Japanese equivalent of a "smiley face."

Our visits with the third graders covered the end of a reading series around a fox story and the beginning of a story-writing unit. The class was reviewing quotation marks (which are brackets in Japanese). The teacher made an effective and enjoyable lesson by creating an on-the-spot readers' theater, which also highlighted the quoted conversational segments.

There followed a model story in preparation for students' writing one of their own. Since students in Japan are given their textbooks, rather than borrowing them, they may write in them. These students marked sections they considered well written and discussed the story at length, especially in terms of the emotions expressed. As homework, begun in class a few days later, students were asked to fill in planning sheets and to make rough drafts of their own stories. For this writing the textbook provided the following story starter: "Deep in the mountains there lived two foxes . . ."

The following day, consulting their rough drafts and planning sheets, each student completed the bulk of a final draft. The teacher walked around, reading over students' shoulders and making suggestions. We overheard her answering a question about when to indent, correcting hand position on the pencil, and reminding the class as a whole about good writing posture. All of these reminders would be less likely in a class in which the students' connection with reality through writing is the primary aim.

The stories, read at random the next day in class, were not uninteresting, but there seemed to have been little gain by requiring the opening phrase. There were several stories about foxes playing soccer and one about traveling to famous places in Japan. These seemed to be stories that students had wanted to write, and they had managed to write them even including the required fox characters, since fantasy was allowed. None were personal experiences (as might be expected, since few of us have known foxes in real life). There was not much commitment to the content that dealt with foxes, but the avid soccer fans wrote vividly about the game aspects of their plots. In the seikatsu format, of course, the story would have included foxes only if the child had some actual connection to express. Students who wanted to write about soccer would not be forced to include references to anything else.

The atmosphere in the sixth-grade class of the same school contrasted sharply with the rowdiness of the first-grade class and the relaxed humor of the third graders. Many children in the sixth grade had begun attending *juku,* after-school cram schools. When *juku* attendance begins, it may drain attention from public-school studies; one sixth-grade teacher described catching students doing their homework on their laps in the midst of his lessons.

The writing unit we watched the sixth graders work on in K-chan's school makes a good parallel to step two writing in the seikatsu five-step plan. Using notebooks and notes they had jotted in the margins of their textbooks, students reported their observations of the emotional changes the main character of a certain story had undergone. It was about a boy who thought he had seen a UFO, but it turned out to be only a large white balloon. (The story was realistic; if it had been a composition known to have been written by an actual child, a seikatsu teacher might have chosen to use it as a motivating piece of writing.) When the teacher asked for interpretation of the key part of the story, the students indicated that the boy was expressing sadness over giving up a childish fantasy in the face of undeniable facts. The teacher asked the students to imagine other "loss of childish belief" situations. One boy suggested that a child could naively mistake a nun for a *ninja* (clandestine warrior) and be disappointed to learn the truth. The teacher alluded to that possibility several times during the ensuing discussion. (A seikatsu teacher would probably have glossed over this imaginative contribution in search of some examples, even if less dramatic, from students' own lives.)

The model composition from the textbook that launched the writing component that followed was a third-person account that described a girl's changing attitudes toward her younger sister over a seven-year period. The introduction to the sample indicated that the author may have based it upon her own life but had simply chosen to tell it as if it were about a character named Yuki. Just as a seikatsu proponent would, the teacher in this class asked students to write their own compositions in the first person. She helped them analyze the sections of the story and the thread that connected these into a theme, "growth of the heart." Her questioning was directed toward the writer's perspective, as if this were a classmate's work instead of a textbook example.

The time allowed for topic choice and planning seemed similar also to that in seikatsu classrooms we attended: four periods of pre-writing. The teacher specified a minimum length of two pages; in seikatsu methodology there is no predetermination of length, but accounts are to be written in detail "just as it was, so we can all understand."

The final two periods of the unit included one self-editing session and another, the following day, given over to group editing. Students passed papers around in groups of four, writing comments and suggesting corrections in round-robin fashion. After group editing, all that remained was for the teacher to evaluate and return the papers.

The educational philosophy represented by language-arts classes in K-chan's school probably prevail in most Japanese elementary schools. There are certainly not many schools whose teachers all claim to adhere to the seikatsu method. Although statistical data are hard to come by, we think that well below ten percent of the students in Japan ever have a seikatsu teacher.

There has been a gradual trend toward including the writing of a short essay as part of college entrance tests. If this catches on, secondary-school teachers will undoubtedly promote more writing in higher education. This will be productive for advanced seikatsu writing as well. At present there are only a small number of active seikatsu teachers beyond elementary-school level, so A-san is unlikely to experience seikatsu training if he did not get any during his elementary years.

A-san is assigned to a homeroom with a homeroom teacher in high school. Except for classes in which special equipment requires the group to move, and for an occasional elective, he is taught with the same group in that classroom during most of the day. The teachers will come to his homeroom for such lessons as history, language arts, and mathematics. A-san may have some teachers who follow his class through the three years of high school in a subject such as language arts.

The seikatsu high-school teacher we visited, Kouda, had been with her class since they began high school. She told us that she had started them with journal writing along with personal narrative compositions, in step one ("a certain day, a certain time") writing. Steps two and three, however, did not need to be taught because explanation and generalization occur naturally in writing by students of this age.

During their second year of high school they had written self-histories; this assignment was intended to get them to look at their lives anew and in light of their emerging perspective of society. One of the particular benefits of writing a self-history at this age, Kouda said, is that this provides students with an excuse to take in the vision of themselves in the real world when they risk having their lives buried under the onus of cramming. The reader issue remains below the surface, even though reader awareness is certainly present in writing by older students. Kouda indicated that she wants to keep reader awareness from becoming reader obsession while writers verify themselves in what they want to express. She has also discovered that students make more progress in writing when they have a self-expressive purpose than when skills are dealt with on a piecemeal basis.

When we visited the class in early July, we observed an appreciation session based upon two essays by students who had agreed to share their writing with their classmates, all now seniors facing "examination hell" in a few months. Kouda believes that the difference between finding only a few good compositions in a mass of poor ones and having almost all students experience success is in the time taken between initial stimulus and the actual writing, so the students had prepared extensively for writing. They had filled in organizational sheets indicating topics, corresponding evidence, their own perspective, points of argument, and sequence. While all this planning goes on, Kouda maintains, there is time for a commitment to the writing to seed itself and grow so that the student has a strong conviction to be expressed when writing takes place.

The first composition was written in response to an article about a child raised by a wolf and dealt with the author's conception of what is meant by humanity. The second composition echoed some of the often-heard arguments for relief from examination pressures as well as regret over the role of education in the ultranationalistic World War II period in Japan. Its author, Mieko Ashida, had written:

. . . Now we are no longer engaged in the kind of war where bombs are dropped, but the kind where human minds are assaulted in an "examination war." Young people are losing their sense of pride, their hearts. Those who educate them, parents and teachers, are making robots out of them for the sake of their own selfish interest, "for the sake of the family," "for the sake of the school," "for the sake of the juku," if not, this time, "for the sake of the state." Education should not be engaged in producing robots.

Elementary schoolchildren wear headbands with the words "Win without fail" and they have an almost-adult look about them. . . .

The writer went on to say that she herself planned to become a teacher and resolved to try to help restore childhood to children as part of her own career.

The seikatsu movement evolved in the face of children's poverty and despair, and flourished in the recognition of the dangers of totalitarianism. Present debates concern mostly the problems of life in a highly competitive society, consumerism and media saturation, the fragmentation of family life, and apathy toward ethical issues. But the object still remains to have children write compositions in the hope that they will attain self-actualization and self-determination. In the face of academic pressures and the bombardment of factual information, seikatsu teachers still insist that students must be encouraged to ask "Why?" even if standardized entrance examinations cannot deal with such thinking.

CONCLUSION

CHAPTER **14** INTERNATIONAL PERSPECTIVES

Throughout this book we have referred to Britton's models, particularly in terms of expressive writing. Touching upon the broad educational implications of such writing, Peter Medway states: "acceptance of the need for expressive language implies a shift to a more equal distribution of power between teacher and taught" (1984:156). Medway calls it a form of language deprivation when school language use has mitigated against students by denying them the opportunity to talk and write in personal modes. The remediation of such school-fostered language deprivation is to start with language that is closest to the child. This can include protecting the child's use of expressive writing as a means of learning in all subjects, hence its association with the writing-across-the-curriculum movement. Medway calls it "ecological" to let students "apply to the content of the disciplines processes of exploring and interpreting akin to those they already use on their life experiences," and says, "it is in effect a human rights issue" (p. 157).

In seikatsu tsuzurikata the valuing of language close to the child includes self-chosen topics and a great deal of control of the writing process because children's authority is assumed in their commitment to the writing. This links seikatsu education with the process approach to teaching writing, described by Murray, Graves, Calkins, and others, especially in terms of ownership of the authoring process.

The issue that underlies the seikatsu philosophy is authenticity in education. Proponents of seikatsu education have not had to emphasize this issue in terms of language use, although they do stress the importance of accepting writing in the child's natural style, including local dialects. Rather, their argument in pre-war Japan was launched against the content aspects of the national curriculum that were incongruent with many of the realities of their students' lives, especially in impoverished areas. Seikatsu teachers were those who simply could not resolve themselves to closing their eyes and teaching the obvious irrelevancies and even contradictory morality of lessons designed predominantly to serve the needs of the state. And today, although Japanese education at compulsory levels is now a model of equality, the overall system of national education is still a strong force toward what Adam Curle would call "belonging-identity" and "competitive materialism." In its overall effects, Japanese education seems less successful at education for personal enrichment than, as Curle would recognize it, "the commodity which enables him to buy into the system" (1973:28). Educational opportunities may be fairly well distributed in Japan, but those opportunities still direct the individual up status-attainment ladders that progressively narrow toward occupational success. The complex of values that accompanies competition in Japan is closely associated with achieving a certain identity, as a graduate of a prestigious school, for example, or an employee of a prosperous company. The seikatsu movement continues to counter this form of delineation by promoting writing that highlights humanistic values, social equality, and appreciation of nature in the face of the impersonal pressures of a technological, consumer-oriented national mentality.

Let us consider what might be compatriotic between a variety of Western philosophical ideals for education and the seikatsu theory and methodology. The quality of effective seikatsu teaching that is mirrored by similar movements elsewhere may be the ability to relate local experience to universal truths. This is the determined search for authenticity that educators, whose dedication begins with the student, share the world over. And the struggle against inauthenticity can be recognized even when its manifestation is unique to a given local context. This cannot be more readily acknowledged than in the home ground of seikatsu philosophy itself, where it was the local needs of children that inspired their teachers to develop the educational aims and practices of the movement in the first place.

The fact that seikatsu education begins and persists in writer bias, honoring language close to the self of the writer, gives this a common grounding with the whole-language movement, which begins and builds upon the strengths and experiences that the student brings to the task. In chapter 16, we indicated how the whole-language movement can be reflected in the seikatsu experience. Like seikatsu proponents, whole-language teachers weave the natural learning processes of students into theory, which then is worked back into practice. The world of the whole-language classroom is a nurturing, mutually contributory milieu in which neither the teacher nor the student holds the trump card that is used to win the game; instead, each facilitates the evolutionary aspect of the learning process so that teachers and students are both, in a sense, learners and teachers. In the same vein, seikatsu educators attempt to avoid fractionating a child's school life; rather, they try to learn from the child's real life and thinking. This is a notable point of affinity with the whole-language movement.

Written language is but one arena of self-awareness and interpersonal appreciation. Since we traditionally associate the skills of reading and writing with the word *literacy*, it is easy to consider seikatsu education to be literacy for self-determination, especially since it also satisfies the traditional objectives of literacy training.

The concept of literacy for self-determination, however, must include many forms of expression. Especially important in many cultures are some of the dramatic attempts to unite relevance and education by engaging students in discussions, interviews, and role play. Debates, group-dynamics exercises, and simulation tasks for problem solving are ways teachers typically encourage students to experience self-awareness through face-to-face interaction. Sometimes these exercises function as pre-writing activities and do lead into writing, but it is intriguing how consistently we in America expect oral expression to be a primary vehicle for real-self discovery. As Americans we seem better able to confront each other orally, and relatively less willing to commit ourselves spontaneously in writing. In Japan, on the other hand, evidence suggests that personal writing is a relatively more comfortable alternative to speaking out (cf. Barnlund 1974, Kurato 1975). There, the opposite sequence is likely to be followed: children keep a journal, discuss writing done by others, write again from their own experience, and then appreciate through discussion the real self of the writer as revealed in the writing. The issue of culture dependency comes into play in self-discovery.

Whatever the culture, there is likely to be a variety of literacy-related media through which the many schemata of self-expression operate. If we define literacy as more than simplistic achievement levels of reading and writing, we come up with a broader concept of literacy in a global frame of reference: literacy for self-determination. Beyond skill-building for purely functional purposes, this form of literacy needs to incorporate all forms of art that function in what Britton refers to as the spectator mode, as transmitters of social reality. Literacy for self-determination would have to encompass oral tradition, such as legends and morality tales as well as dance, art, drama, music, and even humor. In terms of personal development, such literacy fosters the achievement of the inherent social role of the individual without limiting that role or function to society's choice for the person. This is why the scope must include a multiplicity of avenues to self-determination. And this is what the ideals of the seikatsu movement must lead to when viewed in terms of its implications for authentic education worldwide.

Let us use a concrete example, a scene Mary has frequently seen from her classroom window. Near a house across the street three children are at play. One, about seven, is playing the drum with amazing virtuosity. (He had been playing for years, until recently drumming on an upturned wastebasket and boxes.) A child of about four and a toddler no more than two are marching up and down the sidewalk in time to the drum. They carry crudely painted sticks, one long and one short, which they hit together in time with the rhythm. The toddler follows the four-year-old's lead as they turn, pause, proceed, stop, and then run toward the carport, all in excellent imitation of a key ceremony performed months before in the Yaqui Easter ritual of their tribe. It is remarkable that the seven-year-old drums so perfectly, that the four-year-old matches the ceremonial movements so confidently, but most of all, that the toddler performs so diligently *a ceremony he cannot possibly remember seeing.* This re-enactment, in our terms, is an example of literacy for self-determination.

What then, is the role of the school, where non-Yaqui teachers await these three children with curricula and textbooks poised? Can we ignore the richness of this form of literacy because it does not appear in the districtwide guidelines? The tribal leaders prefer to transmit cultural lore themselves and sometimes utilize the school as a convenient setting for language and culture lessons. Besides convenience, however, they use the school setting symbolically, because they hope to improve students' school performance by heightening cultural self-awareness. They too want to cultivate authenticity in education: to say that heritage and collective wisdom and cultural unity are aspects of education is to re-value academic study. The tribal elders and parents want students to acquire the knowledge and certificates of education necessary for employment, but typically these are pupils who do not perform meaningless tasks without personal significance. The dropout rate remains very high among this group, perhaps partly because the system has not included enough of what we are calling literacy for self-determination.

Seikatsu proponents have claimed repeatedly in the history of their movement that their philosophy is not merely one aspect of education, but is instead education itself. It is true that the goal of making a whole person, grounded in reality, at one with nature, mankind, and society (our extrapolation of the values we heard repeatedly in seikatsu circles) is very close to a definition of education itself. While societies often function as self-serving interpreters of how to be "at one with society," a thread that binds idealistic teachers in many parts of the globe is the persistent maintenance of those aims in terms of genuine quality in each individual life.

Seikatsu education is designed to counter education that means nothing to the student. Specifically, this is accomplished by countering writing that means nothing to the writer. Such writing lacks a real-self basis, whether or not its outward form meets the assignment skillfully.

As a form of writing education, seikatsu tsuzurikata provides us with a view of a remarkably fundamental model. The process by which any writer grapples with writer-biased concerns is the foundation of the act of writing. A student of Mary's whom we will call Alberto experienced a great deal of trouble with writing. His pieces seemed to skim rapidly toward conclusions and exhibited a generally unsuccessful struggle to achieve a readably spelled text. Toward the end of the year, however, Alberto's cousin was killed in a particularly gruesome accident. The journal entry Alberto wrote soon after that, describing the terrible scene, was not only detailed, precise, and well-organized, but contained the fewest spelling errors of any of his writing all year. It has to be assumed that the difference lay in the author's commitment to exploring and expressing his topic, as compared to past writing tasks, which to him had been merely exercises.

One of the earmarks of seikatsu writing is that there must be authenticity in author commitment. This is an argument against story starters and assigned topics. If a child has been awake much of the night at a funeral wake or listening anxiously to a parents' quarrel, how can that child write convincingly on the subject "The Day the Circus Came to Town," even if that is the theme of the week? Both oral and written modes of self-discovery can serve as avenues for the engagement of self with reality. And literacy can include nonliterary events that function in the cause of self-determination. Self-determination may best be fostered through written, oral, and even nonverbal expression. We have a variety of traditions in place, but our educational systems tend to value the merits of them unequally.

In this book we have described a system of self-determination literacy that favors solidification of the self through personal writing, first to an intimate audience with an especially strong writer bias, then gradually extending to others. It is important for us as educators in the West to consider including writing for self-discovery into our teaching repertoire of discussion, drama, and collaboration, which come so naturally to many (though not all) societal groups here. Teachers should consider the seikatsu philosophy and methods from the point of view of their own cultural context and educational milieu. But writer-biased processes are a fundamental way to get in touch with that inner text which underlies education itself. And writing for self-discovery complements our flourishing Western composition education programs as well. For all these reasons, it would be mutually beneficial to build bridges of dialogue to connect similar educational philosophies and curricula all over the world.

NOTES

Chapter One: Our Research Base

1. Written by Hiroyuki Katoo, first grade, Ogi Elementary School, Shinshoo City, Yamagata Prefecture, in *Dai Juugokai Jidoo Seito Sakubun Konkuuru Nyuusen Saku* (The Fifteenth Annual Schoolchildren Composition Contest Award Winners), ed. by Shinshoo Shi Kyooiku Iinkai (Shinshoo City Board of Education), 1976, pp. 32–33.
2. Among the bestsellers, we may count the following: *Yamaimo*, ed. by Michio Sagawa, 1951; *Yamabiko Gakkoo*, ed. by Seikyoo Muchaku, 1951; and *Tsuzurikata Kyooshitsu*, by Masako Toyoda, (it has sometimes been debated, however, if the last one cited should properly belong to the category of seikatsu tsuzurikata). *Yamabiko Gakkoo* was made into a movie in 1952, and *Tsuzurikata Kyooshitsu* in 1938.
3. Written by Nakamura (the first name not given by the author), first grade, February 16, 1984, Seikei Elementary School, Tokyo (teacher: Goro Kamemura).

Chapter Two: Writer-Biased Writing Education

1. Written by a first-grade girl soon after the beginning of the school year; quoted in Kamemura (1980:18).
2. Written by Mayuko Inoue, first grade, Funakoshi Elementary School, Yokosuka City (teacher: Sadayuki Tanaka), in *Den Den Mushi* (The Snail), class anthology, vol. 1, p. 66 (1982). The teacher's comment follows the composition immediately on the same page.
3. Written by Masaki Isono, first grade, Funakoshi Elementary School, in *Den Den Mushi*, vol. 1, p. 60 (1982). The teacher's comment follows directly.
4. Written by Yukari Oosawa, third grade, Sannai Elementary School, Aomori City (teacher: Seiichi Hashimoto), in *Gakkyuu Bunshuu Sannai Yama* (Class Anthology Sannai Mountain), vol. 3, pp. 43–44 (1983).
5. Written by Sanae Tsuruta, first grade, Funakoshi Elementary School,

Yokosuka City (teacher, Sadayuki Tanaka), in *Den Den Mushi*, vol. 1, p. 56 (1982). The teacher's comment follows directly.

Chapter Three: The Heart of Seikatsu Writing Education

1. Written by Yasuhide Kawakatsu, quoted in Kamemura (1971:17).
2. Written by Masashi Oono, quoted in Watanabe (1984:101).
3. Written by Hiroki Takahashi, quoted in Kamemura (1971:98–99).

Chapter Four: Language Arts or Self-Actualization?

1. Written by Masami Hamaishi, fourth grade, Oonoura Branch School, Kumamoto Prefecture (teacher: Takamasa Wakiyama), in *Sakubun to Kyooiku* (Composition and Education) 34(12):84–86 (1983).
2. Comment by Shigeki Honma, published in *Sakubun to Kyooiku* 34(12):70–71 (1983).
3. A speech by Michio Namekawa delivered at the third Writing Education Study Conference (1954), entitled "Sakubun no Michi-wa Hitotsu" (The Road of Writing Education is One); see Otobe (1982:99) and Oouchi (1984:221) for the historical background relating to this speech.

Chapter Five: Community Building as an Aim of Seikatsu Writing

1. Written by Kumiko Hara, fifth grade, June 23, 1984, Misaka Elementary School, Nakatsugawa, Gifu Prefecture (teacher: Noriko Niwa).

Chapter Six: A Historical Outline of the Seikatsu Movement

1. Written by Yoshinori Kawai, in Muchaku (1969:213–15).

Chapter Seven: If That Is a Topic, I Have Something to Say Too

1. Written by Etsuko Takahashi, fourth grade, quoted in Kikuchi (1977:105).

Chapter Eight: Journal Writing

1. Written by Toshihito Konagai, quoted in Kamemura (1971:61).
2. Each separate phonetic symbol (*hiragana* letter) represents a syllable in Japanese. For example, the second column from the right in Kaori's composition (Figure 2) would be read as follows, box by box: "*ki yo u no a sa ga k ko u ni ku ru to*" (this morning on the way to school). Unlike English, Japanese is not written with spaces between words.

Chapter Nine: The Akapen

1. Written by Makoto Mori, second grade, Kashiwai Elementary School, Chiba City (teacher: Hiroko Iwatani), in *Hazunde* (Bouncing), the class anthology for 1982–83, p. 49.

Chapter Ten: Four Evaluatory Standards

1. Written by Kazuko Shibata, sixth grade, Hane Elementary School, Okazaki City (teacher: Katsuki Kamura), in *Sakubun to Kyooiku* 34(8):174–78 (1983 Annual Japan Children's Composition and Poem Anthology issue).
2. Written by Katsuyoshi Takeishi, fifth grade, Katsukura Elementary School, Ibaragi Prefecture (teacher: Kiyomi Morita), in *Sakubun to Kyooiku* 34(8):147–49 (1983 Annual Japan Children's Composition and Poem Anthology issue).
3. Written by Tooru Futami, fifth grade, Suda Elementary School, Tokyo (teacher: Moto Takayama), in *Tokyo no Ko* (Children of Tokyo) 9:130–32 (1983). Tokyo: Tokyo Sakubun Kyoogi Kai.

Chapter Eleven: Reality Connection and Writing

1. Quoted in Cleaver (1976:143); from Yasunari Kawabata, *Snow Country*, tr. by Edward G. Seidensticker (New York: Berkley, 1964).
2. Written by Hidetoku Takahashi, *Asahi Journal*, June 8, 1984, p. 95.

Chapter Twelve: Lesson Planning

1. Written by Toyokazu Kobayashi, third grade, March 2, 1984, Kamishizu Elementary School, Sakura City, Chiba Prefecture (teacher: Kazuo Takeda).
2. Written by Naori Sasaki, first grade, March 2, 1984, Kamishizu Elementary School, Sakura City, Chiba Prefecture (teacher: Keiko Yamada).

Chapter Thirteen: Poetry

1. Written by Hidenobu Miyashita, fourth grade, November 8, 1983, Tokiwadaira Elementary School, Matsudo City, Chiba Prefecture (teacher: Hiroshi Tsuzaki).
2. Written by Etsuko Maruyama, third grade, as quoted in Eguchi (1968:248).
3. Written by Nobuhiro Yamamoto, first grade, Machida Elementary School, Tokyo (teacher: Kiyo Sasaki), in *Tokyo no Ko* 9:137.
4. Written by Sumie Murayama, fourth grade, Matsunoyama Elementary School, Niigata Prefecture (teacher: Ryuuhoo Tsubata), in *Shi no Kyooshitsu* (Poetry Classes), school poem anthology, No. 2, p. 3 (1983).
5. Written by Shigeru Kimura, first grade, as quoted in Eguchi (1968:46).

6. Written by Kyooko Kubo, first grade, as quoted in Eguchi (1968:171).
7. Written by Shoogo Kawano, first grade, as quoted in Eguchi (1968:130).
8. Written by Norikazu Oono, second grade, as quoted in Eguchi (1968:132–33).
9. Written by Masanobu Ishii, second grade, as quoted in Eguchi (1968:136).
10. Written by Yuuji Iwahashi, fifth grade, as quoted in Eguchi (1968:137).
11. Written by Nobuko Kutsukake, fifth grade, Shiozaki Elementary School, Nagano City, Nagano Prefecture (teacher: Chitaru Kubota), in *Shiozaki no Ko, Nakagumi no Kodomo-tachi no Shi* (Children of Shiozaki, Poems of the *Naka* Class Children), class anthology, p. 24 (1980).
12. Written by Noriko Sugiyama, second grade, Hane Elementary School, Aichi Prefecture (teacher: Keiko Taguchi), in *Sakubun to Kyooiku* 35(8):52 (1984 Annual Japan Children's Composition and Poem Anthology issue).
13. Written by Yoshishige Nakamura, ninth grade, as quoted in Horisawa (1983:93).
14. Written by Tomoko Ito, first grade, quoted in Nagayasu (1979:120).
15. Translation based on Sagawa (1979:12–13).
16. Translation based on Sagawa (1979:24–25).
17. Translation based on Sagawa (1979:58–62).

Chapter Fourteen: Steps One Through Three

1. Written by Tadashi Watai, first grade, Funakoshi Elementary School, Yokosuka City (teacher: Sadayuki Tanaka), in *Den Den Mushi*, class anthology, vol. 1, p. 31 (1982).
2. As quoted anonymously in Hino (1983:52–53).
3. Written by Yasue Shikano, fifth grade, February 1, 1984, Kita Kaizuka Elementary School, Chiba Prefecture (teacher: Masao Hino).
4. Written by Shin Hattori, third grade, as quoted in Takura (1985:16).
5. Comment by Teruo Tamiya in "Kyoodoo Tooron: Seikatsu Tsuzurikata to wa Nanika" (A Panel Discussion: What Is Seikatsu Tsuzurikata?), *Sakubun to Kyooiku* 27 (12):32–55 (1976), p. 49.
6. Written by Yooko Muramatsu, first grade, Funakoshi Elementary School, Yokosuka City (teacher: Sadayuki Tanaka), in *Den Den Mushi*, vol. 1, p. 65 (1982).
7. Written by Tamiyo Yuda, fifth grade, Horikiri Elementary School, Katsushika-ku, Tokyo (teacher: Noriko Sagawa), in *Sakubun no Kyooiku* 34(8):171–73 (1983 Annual Japan Children's Composition and Poem Anthology issue).
8. Written by Yuuichi Ishikawa, sixth grade, Nisshin Elementary School, Shinshoo City, Yamagata Prefecture, in *Dai Juunanakai Jidoo Seito Sakubun Konkuuru Nyuusen Saku* (The Seventeenth Annual Schoolchildren Composition Contest Award Winners), ed. by

Shinshoo Shi Kyooiku Iinkai (Shinshoo City Board of Education), 1978, pp. 12–13.

9. The composition appears in *Tsubasa* (Wings), class anthology (April 1983–March 1984), pp. 93–94.

10. Written by Takayuki Iwai, sixth grade, as quoted by Nakanishi (1984:95).

Chapter Fifteen: Steps Four and Five

1. Written by Saiko Ozawa, sixth grade, Seikei Elementary School, Musashino City, Tokyo (teacher: Goro Kamemura), in *Sakubun to Kyooiku* 34(8):96–97 (1983 Annual Japan Children's Composition and Poem Anthology issue).

Chapter Sixteen: Seikatsu Curriculum in Light of Language-Arts Education in the West

1. Written by Minoru Shishido, fourth grade, Nogawa Elementary School, Tokyo, as quoted in Inoue (1983:50–52). As is customary for boys his age, Shishido is referred to by his last name in class.

REFERENCES

English References

Barnlund, Dean C. 1974. "The Public Self and the Private Self in Japan and the United States." In *Intercultural Encounters with Japan: Communication—Contact and Conflict*, edited by John C. Condon and Mitsuko Saito, pp. 27–96. Tokyo: The Simul Press.

Britton, James. 1972. "Writing to Learn and Learning to Write." In *The Humanity of English*, pp. 31–53. Urbana, IL: NCTE.

———. 1975a. *Development of Writing Abilities (11–18)* (with Tony Burgess, Nancy Martin, Alex McLeod, and Harold Rosen). London: Macmillan Education.

———. 1975b. "Now That You Go to School." In *Children and Writing in the Elementary School*, edited by Richard L. Larson, pp. 3–16. New York: Oxford University Press.

———. 1977. "Language and the Nature of Learning: An Individual Perspective." In *The Seventy-Sixth Yearbook of the National Society for the Study of Education*, pp. 1–38. Chicago: The University of Chicago Press.

Bruner, Jerome. 1975. "The Ontogenesis of Speech Acts." *Journal of Child Language* 2:1–40.

Cleaver, Charles Grinnell. 1976. *Japanese and Americans: Cultural Parallels and Paradoxes*. Tokyo: Charles E. Tuttle Co.

Cummings, William K. 1980. *Education and Equality in Japan*. Princeton, NJ: Princeton University Press.

Curle, Adam. 1973. *Education for Liberation*. New York: John Wiley & Sons, Inc.

Dore, R. P. 1965. *Education in Tokugawa Japan*. Berkeley and Los Angeles: University of California Press.

Edwards, Betty. 1979. *Drawing on the Right Side of the Brain*. Los Angeles: J. P. Tarcher, Inc.

Flower, Linda. 1979. "Writer-Based Prose: A Cognitive Basis for Problems in Writing." *College English* 41(1):19–37.

Goodman, Kenneth S., and Yetta M. Goodman. 1981. "A Whole-Language Comprehension-Centered View of Reading Development."

Position Paper 1, School of Education, University of Arizona, Tucson, AZ.

Goodman, Yetta M. 1978. "Kidwatching: An Alternative to Testing." *National Elementary Principal* 57(4):41–45.

Graves, Donald H. 1983. *Writing: Teachers and Children at Work*. Portsmouth, NH: Heinemann Educational Books.

Kelly, George A. 1955. *The Psychology of Personal Constructs*, Vol. 1, New York: W. W. Norton & Co.

Kitagawa, Mary M. 1982. "Expressive Writing in Japanese Elementary Schools." *Language Arts* 59(1):18–22.

Kurato, Yoshiya. 1975. "A Feasibility Study for Measuring the Intensity of Self-Disclosure between American and Japanese Populations. Ph.D. diss., University of Massachusetts, Amherst.

Macrorie, Ken. 1980. *Searching Writing*. Upper Montclair, NJ: Boynton/ Cook Publishers.

Medway, Peter. 1984. "The Bible and the Vernacular: The Significance of Language Across the Curriculum." In *English Teaching, An International Exchange*, edited by James Britton, pp. 153–57. London and Portsmouth, NH: Heinemann Educational Books.

Moffett, James. 1983. "Rationale for a New Curriculum in English." In *Theory and Practice in the Teaching of Composition: Processing, Distancing, and Modeling*, ed. by Miles Myers and James Gray, pp. 150–58. Champaign, IL: National Council for Teachers of English. (Originally published in 1967 in *Rhetoric: Theories for Application*, ed. by Robert M. Gorrell, pp. 114–21. Champaign, IL: National Council for Teachers of English.)

Murray, Donald. 1984. "On the Cutting Edge of Writing." *Today's Education* (1984 National Education Association Newsletter), pp. 54–55.

Nakamura, Hajime. 1967. "Consciousness of the Individual and the Universal Among the Japanese." In *The Japanese Mind*, edited by Charles A. Moore, pp. 179–200. Honolulu: East-West Center Press.

Passin, Herbert. 1982. *Society and Education in Japan*. Tokyo: Kodansha International. (First published by the Teachers College Press, Columbia University, in 1965.)

Uyeno, Tazuko. 1971. "A Study of Japanese Modality—A Performative Analysis." Ph.D. diss., University of Michigan.

Vygotsky, L. S. 1962. *Thought and Language*. Cambridge, MA: MIT Press.

Winter, Prescott B. 1982. "Language, Thought and Institutions in Tokugawa Japan." Ph.D. diss., Stanford University.

Japanese References

Asahina, Terumoto. 1976. *Kokugo Kyooiku, Gonensei* (Language Arts, Fifth Grade). Tokyo: Ayumi Shuppan.

Ashida, Enosuke. 1913. *Tsuzurikata Kyooju* (The Teaching of Tsuzurikata). Tokyo: Koogeikan.

Eguchi, Sueyoshi. 1968. *Jidooo Shi Kyooiku Nyuumon* (Introduction to Poetry Education). Tokyo: Yuri Shuppan.

Hanaoka, Masae. 1980. "Seikatsu ni Fukaku Nezashita Kyooiku o

Motomete" (Searching for Education Rooted in the Real-Life Context). In *Naze Seikatsu Tsuzurikata o Eranda Ka* (Why Did I Choose Seikatsu Tsuzurikata?), edited by Akiomi Ohta, pp. 8–44. Tokyo: Meiji Tosho.

Hino, Masao. 1983. "Ichinensei no Tanoshii Kijutsu Shidoo" (A Fun Writing Class for the First Graders). *Sakubun to Kyooiku* (Composition and Education) 34(5):48–55.

Horisawa, Toshio. 1983. "Kodomo no Seikatsu no Rizumu o Hikidasu, Chuugakusei no Seikatsu no Shi" (To Help Young People Articulate Their Life Rhythm, Life Experience Poems of Junior High Students). *Sakubun to Kyooiku* 34(13):86–96.

Imai, Kakujiro. 1961. "Bunshoo Hyoogen Keitai no Kiso" (The Foundation of Writing). In *Seikatsu Tsuzurikata no Shidoo Taikei III* (The Seikatsu Tsuzurikata Curriculum III), *Kooza Seikatsu Tsuzurikata* (Seikatsu Tsuzurikata Series), edited by Kakujiroo Imai, Ichitaroo Kokubun, Michio Sagawa, and Michio Namekawa, pp. 13–39. Tokyo: Yuri Shuppan.

Imai, Kakujiro, and Mitsushige Minechi. 1957. *Gakushuu Shidoo no Ayumi, Sakubun Kyooiku* (Composition Education, Along Curriculum Guidance). Tokyo: Tooyoo-kan.

Inoue, Tatsumi. 1983. "Aru Hi Aru Toki no Sensei ya Tomodachi to no Koto de, Kokoro ni Nokotte Iru Koto o Yoku Omoidashite Kaku" (To Write Remembering Well What Has Remained in Your Mind about Teachers and Friends on a Certain Day at a Certain Time). *Sakubun to Kyooiku* 34(10):48–56.

Isoda, Kazuo. 1980. "Seikatsu Tsuzurikata Ronsoo" (Debates on Seikatsu Tsuzurikata). In *Nihon Kyooiku Ronsoo Shi Roku* (Japan Educational Debates Documents), pp. 213–25. Tokyo: Dai Ichi Hooki.

Kamemura, Goro. 1971. *Nikki Shidoo* (Journal Guidance). Tokyo: Yuri Shuppan.

———. 1979. *Akapen no Kakikata* (Writing Akapen). Tokyo: Yuri Shuppan.

———. 1980. *Kodomo-o Ikasu Sakuhin Kyooiku* (Writing Education to Make Children Grow). Tokyo: Yuri Shuppan.

Kawaguchi, Yukihiro. 1980. *Seikatsu Tsuzurikata Kenkyuu* (Study of Seikatsu Tsuzurikata). Tokyo: Shiraishi Shoten.

Kikuchi, Kunio. 1977. "Keikaku-teki Taikei-teki Shidoo no Jissai" (Application of Planned and Systematic Guidance). In *Seikatsu Tsuzurikata no Kiso Kooza* (Lectures on the Fundamentals of Seikatsu Tsuzurikata), pp. 77–119. Tokyo: Shinhyooron.

Kokubun, Ichitaro. 1952. *Atarashii Tsuzurikata Kyooshitsu* (New Tsuzurikata Classroom). Tokyo: Shin Hyooron. (Originally published by Nihon Hyooron, Tokyo, in 1951.)

———. 1982. *Gendai Tsuzurikata no Dentoo to Soozoo* (The Tradition and Creation of Seikatsu Tsuzurikata). Tokyo: Yuri Shuppan.

———. 1984a. "Dai Yon Shidoo Dankai ni Tsuite" (On Step 4). *Sakubun to Kyooiku* 35(2):92–96.

———. 1984b. "Dai Go Shidoo Dankai to Owari no Tsuketari ni Tsuite" (On Step 5 and Addendum). *Sakubun to Kyooiku* 35(3):94–98.

———. 1984c. *Syoogakkoo Kyooshi-tachi no Yuuzai, Kaisoo: Seikatsu*

Tsuzurikata Jiken (The Guilt of Elementary-School Teachers, Recollection: The Seikatsu Tsuzurikata Incident). Tokyo: Misuzu Shoboo.

Muchaku, Seikyoo, ed. 1969. *Yamabiko Gakkoo* (Mountain Echo School). Tokyo: Kadokawa Shoten. (Originally published by Seidoosha, Tokyo, 1951. A portion of this book was translated by Genevieve Caulfield and Michiko Kimura and published by Kenkyuu-sha in 1953 under the title *Echoes from a Mountain School*.)

Nagayasu, Minoru, et al. 1979. "Sakubun to Shi no Jikan" (Time for Composition and Poem). *Sakubun to Kyooiku* 30(7):117–47.

Nakai, Kiyoshi. 1979. "Watashi ni okeru Yoshin Shirabe no Jittai" (The Facts Concerning the Pre-trial Examinations for My Case). *Seikatsu Tsuzurikata* (6):124–45.

Nakajima, Reiko. 1984. "Ima Kodomo-tachi ni Kakaneba-naranu koto o Kakaseru to wa, 1" (Having Children Write What They Need to Write, 1). *Tsuzurikata Tokyo* 1:30–35.

Nakanishi, Hitoshi. 1984. "Genzai Shinkoo Keitai no Hyoogen ni Tsuite Kangaeru" (Notes on Present Progressive Forms). *Sakubun to Kyooiku* 35(1):94–105.

Nakauchi, Toshio. 1977. *Seikatsu Tsuzurikata Seiritsu Shi Kenkyuu* (A Historical Study on the Formation of Seikatsu Tsuzurikata). Tokyo: Meiji Tosho.

———. 1982. *Seikatsu Tsuzurikata*. Tokyo: Kokudo-sha.

Namekawa, Michio. 1977. *Nihon Sakubun Tsuzurikata Kyooiku Shi 1, Meiji-hen* (The History of Writing Education in Japan, 1: The Meiji Period). Tokyo: Kokudo-sha.

———. 1978. *Nihon Sakubun Tsuzurikata Kyooiku Shi 2, Taishoo-hen* (The History of Writing Education in Japan, 2: The Taisho Period). Tokyo: Kokudo-sha.

———. 1983. *Nihon Sakubun Tsuzurikata Kyooiku Shi 3, Shoowa-hen* I (The History of Writing Education in Japan, 3: The Showa Period I). Tokyo: Kokudo-sha.

Niwa, Noriko. 1982. *Asu ni Mukatte* (Toward Tomorrow), Vol. 1. Tokyo: Soodo Bunka.

Nona, Ryuuji. 1983. *Tsuzurikata Kyooiku Ron* (Theory of Composition Education). Tokyo: Ayumi Shuppan.

Otobe, Takeshi. 1982. "'Seikatsu Tsuzurikata' to 'Sakubun Kyooiku'" ("Seikatsu Tsuzurikata" and "Composition Education"). *Sakubun to Kyooiku* 33(5):93–102.

Ouchi, Zen-Ichi. 1984. *Sengo Sakubun Kyooiku Shi Kenkyuu* (The History of Writing Education after the War). Tokyo: Kyooiku Shuppan Center.

Sagawa, Michio. 1951. "Sensei to Kodomo to Seikatsu" (Teachers, Children, and Life). *Jissen Kokugo* (Language Arts in Action) 1951, no. 8 (as quoted in Ouchi 1984:148).

———. 1979. *Oozeki Matsusaburoo Shi Shuu, Yamaimo* (*Yamaimo*, A Collection of Poems by Matsusaburoo Oozeki). Tokyo: Koodansha. (Originally published by Yuri Shuppan, Tokyo, in 1951.)

Sasai, Hideo. 1981. *Seikatsu Tsuzurikata Seisei Shi* (Genesis of Seikatsu Tsuzurikata). Tokyo: Ayumi Shuppan.

Shima, Yoogo. 1984. *Seikatsu Tsuzurikata to Kyooiku* (Seikatsu Tsuzurikata and Education). Tokyo: Aoki Shoten.

Takahashi, Rokusuke. 1936. *Jinseika to shite no Tsuzurikata Keiei no Tenkai* (Development of Composition Management as a Curriculum on Real-Life Education). Tokyo: Bun'ensha.

Takura, Keiichi. 1985. "Sono Toki no Yoosu ya, Kimochi o, Sono Mama Kaku Imi o Kangaeru" (Considering the Meaning of Writing Exactly as It Happened and as It Felt). *Sakubun to Kyooiku* 36(2):14–23.

Tamiya, Teruo. 1968. *Seikatsu Tsuzurikata Kyooiku no Naiyoo to Hoohoo* (The Content and Method of Seikatsu Tsuzurikata Education). Tokyo: Yuri Shuppan.

————. 1983. "Ima, Tashikamete Oku Koto, Akiraka ni Suru Koto" (What We Should Affirm and Clarify Now). *Sakubun to Kyooiku* 34(7):17–26.

Tanaka, Sadayuki. 1984. "Dai San Shidoo Dankai ni Tsuite, 3" (On the Third Step, 3). *Sakubun to Kyooiku* 35(1):87–93.

Taroora, Shin. 1983. "Seikatsu Tsuzurikata Kyooiku Shi Kenkyuu ni okeru 'Seikatsu Tsuzurikata' Kitei no Kentoo" (Examination of the Definition of "Seikatsu Tsuzurikata" in Historical Studies on Seikatsu Tsuzurikata Education). *Tsukuba Daigaku-in Hakase Katei Kyooiku-gaku Kenkyuu Shuuroku* (Studies in Educational Theories, Tsukuba University Doctoral Programs) 7:31–43.

Toyota, Masako. 1937. *Tsuzurikata Kyooshitu* (The Composition Classroom). Tokyo: Chuuoo Kooron Sha.

Tsurumi, Shunsuke. 1956. "Nihon no Puragumatizumu, Seikatsu Tsuzurikata Undoo" (Japanese Pragmatism, the Seikatsu Tsuzurikata Movement). In O. Kuno and S. Tsurumi, *Gendai Nihon Shisoo, Sono Itsutsu no Uzu* (The Modern Japanese Thought, Its Five Currents), pp. 71–115. Tokyo: Iwanami Shoten.

Watanabe, Misako. 1984. "E kara Bun e" (From a Picture to a Composition). *Sakubun to Kyooiku* 35(5):100–104.

INDEX OF WRITING SAMPLES

INDEX OF NAMES AND SUBJECTS

War period in Japan (1931–45), 43; teacher arrests during, 44
Whole-language movement, 136, 164
Winter, Prescott, 129
Writer bias, 11, 13, 15, 18–19, 20–21, 22, 54, 56, 57, 70, 84, 85, 93, 96, 97, 111, 117, 130, 135, 136, 138, 139, 145, 146–47, 164, 167
Writer-biased and reader-biased prose compared (table), 18–19
Writing as making connections (definition of *tsuzurikata*), 6; to anchor experience, 12, 137; with experiencer-self, 17, 93, 124; reading to appreciate, 13–14; with reality, 17–18, 77, 81, 83, 117, 156

Yamabiko Gakkoo (Mountain Echo School): book, 44–47; movie, 46, 169
Yamada, Keiko, 93–94
Yamaimo (Mountain Tuber) book, 45; poems from, 108–10
Yaqui culture, 141, 146–47, 165–66
Yohaku (the remaining white), 100–101

Zen: influence on Ashida, 54